My Reading Life

Also by Pat Conroy
Available from Random House
Large Print

===

My Losing Season
The Pat Conroy Cookbook
South of Broad

PAT CONROY

MY READING LIFE

DRAWINGS BY WENDELL MINOR

RANDOM HOUSE
LARGE PRINT

This book is dedicated to my lost daughter, Susannah Ansley Conroy. Know this: I love you with my heart and always will. Your return to my life would be one of the happiest moments I could imagine.

CONTENTS

CONTENTS

My Reading Life

THE LILY

Between the ages of six and nine, I was a native son of the marine bases of Cherry Point and Camp Lejeune in the eastern coastal regions of North Carolina. My father flew in squadrons of slant-winged Corsairs, which I still think of as the most beautiful warplanes that ever took to the sky. For a year Dad flew with the great Boston hitter and left fielder Ted Williams, and family lore has it that my mother and Mrs. Williams used to bathe my sister and me along with Ted Williams's daughter. That still remains the most distinguished moment of my commonplace career as an athlete. I followed Ted Williams's pursuit of greatness, reveling in my father's insider knowledge that "Ted [has] the best reflexes of any marine pilot who ever flew Corsairs." I read every book about baseball in the library of each base and town we entered, hoping for any information about "the Kid" or "the Splendid Splinter." When the movie of **The Great Santini** came out starring Robert Duvall, Ted Williams told a sportswriter that he'd once flown with Santini. My whole writing career was affirmed with that single, transcendent moment.

The forests around Cherry Point and Camp Lejeune were vast to the imagination of a boy. Once I climbed an oak tree as high as I could go in Camp Lejeune, then watched a battalion of marines with their weapons locked and loaded slip in wordless silence beneath me as they approached enemy territory. When I built a bridge near "B" building in Cherry Point, I invited the comely Kathleen McCadden to witness my first crossing. I had painted my face like a Lumbee Indian and wielded a Cherokee tomahawk I had fashioned to earn a silver arrow point as a Cub Scout. My bridge collapsed in a heap around me and I fell into the middle of a shallow creek as poor Kathleen screamed with laughter on the bank. Though a failed bridge maker, I showed more skill in the task of the tomahawk and I felled Kathleen with a wild toss that deflected off her shoulder blade. My mother handled the whipping that night, so further discipline by my father proved unnecessary. For the rest of my life, I would read books on Native Americans and I once coached an Indian baseball team on the Near North Side of Omaha, Nebraska, after my freshman year at The Citadel. Pretty Kathleen McCadden never spoke to me again, and her father always looked as if he wanted to beat me. I was seven years old.

Yet an intellectual life often forms in the strangest, most infertile of conditions. The deep forests of those isolated bases became the kingdom that I took ownership of as a child. I followed the minnow-laced streams as they made their cutting way toward the Trent River. Each time in the woods, I brought my nature-obsessed mother a series of captured animals, from snapping turtles to copperheads. Mom would study their scales or fur or plumage as I brought home everything from baby herons to squirrels for her patient inspection. After she looked over the day's catch, she would shower me with praise, then send me back into the woods to return my captives where I'd discovered them. She told me she thought I could become a world-class naturalist, or even the director of the San Diego Zoo.

At the library she began to check out books that gave me a working knowledge of those creatures that my inquisitive, overprotective dog and I had found while wandering the woods. When Chippie jumped between me and an eastern diamondback rattler and took a strike on the muzzle before she broke the snake's back, my mother decided that

I'd do my most important work in the game preserves of Africa with the scent of lions inflaming Chippie's extraordinary sense of smell. By the time I had finished fifth grade, I knew the name of almost every mammal in Africa. I even brought her a baby fox once and had a coral snake in a pickle jar. She answered me with trips to the library, where I found a whole section labeled "Africa," the books oversized and swimming with photographs of creatures with their claws extended and their fangs bared. Elephants moved across parched savannas and hippopotamuses bellowed in the Nile River; crocodiles sunned themselves on riverbanks where herds of zebra came to drink their fill. Books permitted me to embark on dangerous voyages to a world of painted faces of mandrills and leopards scanning the veldt from the high branches of a baobab tree. There was nothing my mother could not bring me from a library. When I met a young marine in the woods one day hunting butterflies with a net and a killing jar, my mother checked out a book that took me far into the world of lepidoptera, with hairstreaks, sulphurs, and fritillaries placed in solemn rows.

Whatever prize I brought out of the woods, my mother could match with a book from the library. She read so many books that she was famous among the librarians in every town she entered. Since she did not attend college, she looked to librarians as her magic carpet into a serious intellectual life. Books contained powerful amulets that could lead to paths of certain wisdom. Novels taught her everything she needed to know about the mysteries and uncertainties of being human. She was sure that if she could find the right book, it would reveal what was necessary for her to become a woman of substance and parts. She outread a whole generation of officers' wives but still wilted in embarrassment when asked about her college degree. I was a teenager when I heard Mom claim that she had just finished her first year at Agnes Scott when she dropped out to marry my father. By the time I graduated from The Citadel, my mother was saying that she had matriculated with honors from Agnes Scott, with a degree in English. Though I feared the possibility of her exposure, I thought that the lie was harmless enough. Her vast reading provided all the armor she needed to camouflage her lack of education. At formal teas, she talked of Pasternak and Dostoyevsky. She subscribed to the **Saturday Review,** then passed it on to my sister Carol and me after she had read it from cover to cover. After Mom fell in love with John Ciardi, I checked out his translation of Dante's **The Divine Comedy**. She spoke about the circles of Hell for the rest of her life. Even if Dante daunted and intimidated her, she cherished Eudora Welty and Edith Wharton and knew her way around the works of Hemingway and Fitzgerald. Whenever she opened a new book, she could escape the exhausting life of a mother of seven and enter into cloistered realms forbidden to a woman born among the mean fields of Georgia.

Peg Conroy used reading as a text of liberation, a way out of the sourceless labyrinth that devoured poor Southern girls like herself. She directed me to every book I ever read until I graduated from the eighth grade at Blessed Sacrament School in Alexandria, Virginia. When I won the Martin T. Quinn Scholarship for Academic Achievement, Mom thought she had produced a genius in the rough.

In high school, my mother surrendered my education up to the English teachers who would lead me blindfolded toward the astonishments that literature had to offer. In Belmont, North Carolina, Sister Mary Ann of the Order of the Sacred Heart taught a small but serious class in that Book of Common Prayer that makes up the bulk of a fourteen-year-old American's introduction to the great writers of the world. It took me six months to fathom the mystery that my mother was copying out my homework assignments in an act of mimicry that made me pity her in some ways but admire her indefatigable trek toward self-improvement in others. It was a year my father made dangerous for me, and there was a strange correlation between his brutality and my reaching puberty that was then incomprehensible to me. It infuriated him when he found my mother and me discussing an Edgar Allan Poe short story or Ambrose Bierce's "An Occurrence at Owl Creek Bridge." He found me showing off and vain. It marked the year my blue eyes began to burn with hatred whenever he entered a room. Though I tried, I could not control that loathing no matter what strategies I used. He would take me by the throat in that tiny house on Kees Road, lift me off my feet, strangle me and beat my head against the wall. When later I was living by myself in Atlanta in 1979, my father came to visit me after an extended visit with all his children. He recounted a story that my brother Jim had told him, and said, "Jesus, my kids can make shit up. Jim claimed that his first memory of you was me beating your brains out against some wall. Isn't that hilarious?"

"I can show you the wall," I said.

On the day Sister Mary Ann handed out copies of Shakespeare's **Twelfth Night,** I understood at last that I was coming face-to-face with the greatest writer who ever lived. The strangeness of Elizabethan dialogue stymied me at first, but I was taking turns reading it with my mother, and noted her own puzzlement as we encountered a diction and elaborate phrasing that was unfamiliar to us. When Orsino opens the play with his famous declaration, "If music be the food of love, play on," we were fine, but both of us were stopped in midsentence by a word unknown to us—"surfeiting."

"Look it up, Pat," Mom said. "If we don't know a word, we can't understand the sentence."

I looked up the word and said, "You eat too much. You get too full."

"Like the radio, if they play a song too much, you get sick of it. It happened to me with 'Tennessee Waltz,'" she said.

The next stoppage of our kitchen performance took place when the servant Curio asked the duke if he would go hunting the "hart."

"Maybe it's a misprint," Mom said. "What does it mean?"

"In England it's a deer. A red deer," I said, consulting the dictionary.

"Okay, the duke says that music is the food of love," she said. "I got it. It's a pun. A pun! The duke is in love, so he's going to be hunting the human heart of a young woman."

I've never been a great admirer of the pun, so I didn't quite catch my mother's drift because there lives a strange literalist inside me who swats away at puns as though routing a swarm of flies. It's hard to take pleasure in something you don't understand and in my own psyche, a "hart" could never pass for a "heart." But looking back at the play I haven't read for fifty years, it strikes me now that my mother was correct in her assessment of the Shakespearean world. For the rest of my high school and college career, she read every short story, poem, play, and novel that I read. I would bring notebooks home from The Citadel, and Mom would devour those of each literature course I took. Only after her death did I realize that my mother entered The Citadel the same day I did. She made sure that her education was identical to mine. She knew Milton's **Paradise Lost** a whole lot better than I did.

In my junior year, she developed a school-girl crush on Col. James Harrison, who taught American literature. He filled his lectures with a refined erudition, a passion for good writing, and a complete dedication to the task of turning his cadets into well-spoken and clear-thinking young men. But Mom fell head over heels for the lovely man the day Colonel Harrison read the Whitman poem "When Lilacs Last in the Dooryard Bloom'd." With the softest of voices, he read to his class the poet's moving elegy on the death of Abraham Lincoln. Halfway through his recitation, he confessed to us that he always wept whenever he read that particular poem. He apologized to the class for his lack of professionalism. He wiped his glasses and, with tears streaming down his face, he dismissed the class and headed toward his office. The grandson of a Confederate officer had been moved to tears by a poem commemorating the assassination of Abraham Lincoln. For me that day will last forever. I had no idea that poetry could bring a grown man to his knees until Colonel Harrison proved it. It ratified a theory of mine that great writing could sneak up on you, master of a thousand disguises: prodigal kinsman, messenger boy, class clown, commander of artillery, altar boy, lace maker, exiled king, peacemaker, or moon goddess. I had witnessed with my own eyes that a poem made a colonel cry. Though it was not part of a lesson plan, it imparted a truth that left me spellbound. Great words, arranged with cunning and artistry, could change the perceived world for some readers. From the beginning I've searched out those writers unafraid to stir up the emotions, who entrust me with their darkest passions, their most indestructible yearnings, and their most soul-killing doubts. I trust the great novelists to teach me how to live, how to feel, how to love and hate. I trust them to show me the dangers I will encounter on the road as I stagger on my own troubled passage through a complicated life of books that try to teach me how to die.

I take it as an article of faith that the novels I've loved will live inside me forever. Let me call on the spirit of Anna Karenina as she steps out onto the train tracks of Moscow in the last minute of her glorious and implacable life. Let me beckon Madame Bovary to issue me a cursory note of warning whenever I get suicidal or despairing as I live out a life too sad by half. If I close my eyes I can conjure up a whole country of the dead who will live for all time because writers turned them into living flesh and blood. There is Jay Gatsby floating face downward in his swimming pool or Tom Robinson's bullet-riddled body cut down in his Alabama prison yard in **To Kill a Mockingbird**.

Hector can still impart lessons about honor as he rides out to face Achilles on the plains of Troy. At any time, night or day, I can conjure up the fatal love of Romeo for the raven-haired Juliet. The insufferable Casaubon dies in **Middlemarch** and Robert Jordan awaits his death in the mountains of Spain in **For Whom the Bell Tolls**. In **Look Homeward, Angel,** the death of Ben Gant can still make me weep, as can the death of Thomas Wolfe's stone-carving father in **Of Time and the River**. On the isle of Crete I bought **Report to Greco** by Nikos Kazantzakis and still see the immortal scene when the author's father took him to a devastated garden to witness the swinging bodies of Greek patriots hanging from the branches of fruit trees. In a scene that has haunted me since I first read it, the father lifted his son off the Cretan earth and made the boy kiss the bottom of the dead men's feet. Though nearly gagging, the young Kazantzakis kisses dirt from the lifeless feet as the father tells him that's what courage tastes like, that's what freedom tastes like.

When Isabel Archer falls in love with Gilbert Osmond in **The Portrait of a Lady,** I still want to signal her to the dangers inherent in this fatal choice of a husband, one whose cunning took on an attractive finish but lacked depth. She has chosen a man whose character was not only undistinguished, but also salable to the highest bidder.

To my mother, a library was a palace of desire masquerading in a wilderness of books. In the downtown library of Orlando, Florida, Mom pointed out a solid embankment of books. In serious battalions the volumes stood in strict formations, straight-backed and squared away. They looked like unsmiling volunteers shined and ready for dress parade. "What furniture, what furniture!" she cried, admiring those books looking out on a street lined with palms and hibiscus.

I was eleven years old that year, and my brother Jim was an infant. Mom walked her brood of six children along the banks of Lake Eola on the way home to Livingston Street. My uncle Russ would leave his dentist's office at five, pick up the books my mother had checked out for herself and her kids, and hand-deliver them on his way home to North Hyer Street. On this particular day, Mom stopped with her incurious children near an artist putting the finishing touches on a landscape illuminating one corner of the park surrounding the lake. She gazed at the painting with a joyful intensity as the artist painted a snow-white lily on a footprint-shaped pad as a final, insouciant touch. Mom squealed with pleasure and the bargaining began. From the beginning, the Florida artist Jack W. Lawrence was putty in my comely mother's hands. Flirtation was less of an art form with her than it was a means to an end, or a way of life. Jack demanded fifty dollars for his masterwork and after much charming repartee between artist and customer, he let it go for ten.

That painting hangs in my writing room today. I am staring at the singular lily nesting like a dove in that ethereal place where my mother purchased her first work of art in 1956 in a backwater city dimpled with lakes. The next week, she checked out large art books from the library and spread them out for Carol and me and read out names seething with musicality and strangeness. A library could show you everything if you knew where to look. Jack W. Lawrence led my mother, who led her children to Giotto, the shepherd, to Michelangelo of the Sistine Chapel, to Raphael and his exquisite Madonnas. Years later, I took Mom to the Vatican Library and a tour of the Sistine Chapel; then we visited the tomb of Raphael at the Pantheon. As we spoke of Raphael, she remembered the book she checked out on the Renaissance in that Florida library. We remembered our chance encounter with Mr. Lawrence and our awed eyewitness to that final, emblematic lily.

My mother hungered for art, for illumination, for some path to lead her to a shining way to call her own. She lit signal fires in the hills for her son to feel and follow. I tremble with gratitude as I honor her name.

CHAPTER TWO

GONE WITH THE WIND

The novel **Gone with the Wind** shaped the South I grew up in more than any other book. During my childhood, my mother bought countless copies to hand out as gifts or to replace the ones she read so frequently that they came apart in her hands. Few white Southerners, even today, can read this book without conjuring up a complex, tortured dreamscape of the South handed down by generations of relatives who grew up with the taste of defeat, like the bluing of gunmetal, still in their mouths. What Margaret Mitchell caught so perfectly was the sense of irredeemable loss and of a backwater Camelot corrupted by the mannerless intrusions of insensate invaders. The Tara invoked in the early chapters of this book is the wistful image of a Southern utopia, a party at Twelve Oaks that might have gone on forever if the hot-blooded boys of the South could have stemmed the passions of secession and held their fire at Fort Sumter. It is the South as an occupied nation that forms the heart

of this not impartial novel. This is **The Iliad**
with a Southern accent, burning with the humiliation of Reconstruction. It is the song of
the fallen, unregenerate Troy, the one sung in
a lower key by the women who had to pick
up the pieces of a fractured society when
their sons and husbands returned with their
cause in their throats, when the final battle
cry was sounded. It is the story of war told by
the women who did not lose it and who refused to believe in its results long after the occupation had begun. According to Margaret
Mitchell, the Civil War destroyed a civilization of unsurpassable amenity, chivalry, and
grace. To Southerners like my mother, **Gone
with the Wind** was not just a book; it was an
answer, a clenched fist raised to the North, an
anthem of defiance. If you could not defeat
the Yankees on the battlefield, then by God,
one of your women could rise from the ashes
of humiliation to write more powerfully than
the enemy and all the historians and novelists
who sang the praises of the Union. The novel
was published in 1936 and it still stands as
the last great posthumous victory of the Confederacy. It will long be a favorite book of any
country that ever lost a war. It is still one of
the most successful novels ever published in
our republic.

    Gone with the Wind is as controversial

a novel as it is magnificent. Even after its publication year, then after Margaret Mitchell won a Pulitzer Prize, the book attracted a glittering array of literary critics, including Malcolm Cowley and Bernard DeVoto, who attacked the artistry and politics of the novel with a ferocity that continues to this day. Margaret Mitchell was a partisan of the first rank and there never has been a defense of the plantation South so implacable in its cold righteousness or its resolute belief that the wrong side had surrendered at Appomattox Court House. In this book, the moral weight of the narrative is solidly and iconoclastically in line with the gospel according to the Confederate States. It stands in furious counterpoint to Harriet Beecher Stowe's **Uncle Tom's Cabin,** which Margaret Mitchell ridicules on several occasions by scoffing at Stowe's famous scene of bloodhounds pursuing runaway slaves across ice floes.

Margaret Mitchell writes of the Confederacy as paradise, as the ruined garden looked back upon by a stricken and exiled Eve, disconsolate with loss. If every nation deserves its own defense and its own day in the sunshine of literature, then Margaret Mitchell rose to the task of playing the avenging angel for the Confederate States. There have been hundreds of novels about the Civil War, but

Gone with the Wind stands like an obelisk in the dead center of American letters casting its uneasy shadow over all of us. It hooked into the sweet-smelling attar that romance always lends to the cause of a shamed and defeated people. Millions of Southerners lamented the crushing defeat of the Southern armies, but only one had the talent to place that elegiac sense of dissolution on the white shoulders of the most irresistible, spiderous, seditious, and wonderful of American heroines, Scarlett O'Hara.

Gone with the Wind is a war novel, a historical romance, a comedy of manners, a bitter lamentation, a cry of the heart, and a long, coldhearted look at the character of this lovely, Machiavellian Southern woman. It is beautifully constructed into fine, swiftly moving parts and sixty-three chapters. Margaret Mitchell possessed a playwright's ear for dialogue and the reader never becomes confused as the hundreds of characters move in and out of scenes throughout the book. She grants each character the clear imprimatur of a unique and completely distinct voice. Once Miss Mitchell has limned the outlines of the main characters, they live eternally in the imagination of the reader. She was born to be a novelist, but then withdrew, having given voice to the one novel bursting along the seams of consciousness. Margaret Mitchell sings her own song of a land-proud, war-damaged South, and her voice is operatic, biblical, epic. Her genius lay in her choice of locale and point of focus and heroine. She leaves the great battlefields of Gettysburg and Vicksburg, Bull Run and Antietam to the others and places the Civil War in the middle of Scarlett O'Hara's living room. She has the Northern cannons sounding beyond Peachtree Creek as Melanie Wilkes goes into labor, and has the city of Atlanta in flames as Scarlett is seized with an overpowering urge to return home that finds her moving down Peachtree Street with the world she grew up in turning to ash around her.

The book begins and ends with Tara, but it is Scarlett herself who represents the unimaginable changes that the war has wrought on all Southerners. It was in Southern women that the deep hatred the war engendered came to nest for real in the years of Reconstruction. The women of the South became the only American women to know the hard truths of war firsthand. They went hungry just as their men did on the front lines in Virginia and Tennessee, they starved when these men failed to come home for four straight growing seasons, and hunger was an old story when the war finally ended. The men of Chancellorsville, Franklin, and the Wilderness seemed to have left some residue of fury on the smoking, blood-drenched fields of battle, whose very names became sacred in the retelling. But Southern women, forced to live with that defeat, had to build granaries around the heart to store the poisons that the glands of rage produced during that war and its aftermath. The Civil War still feels personal in the South, and what the women of the South brought to peacetime was Scarlett O'Hara's sharp memory of exactly what they had lost.

With the introduction of Scarlett O'Hara and Rhett Butler, Miss Mitchell managed to create the two most famous lovers in the English-speaking world since Romeo and Juliet. Scarlett springs alive in the first sentence of the book and holds the narrative center for more than a thousand pages. She is a fabulous, one-of-a-kind creation, and she does not utter a dull line in the entire book. She makes her uncontrollable self-centeredness seem like the most charming thing in the world and one feels she would be more than a match for Anna Karenina, Lady Macbeth, or any of Tennessee Williams's women. Her entire nature shines with the joy of being pretty and sought after and frivolous in the first chapters and we see her character darkening slowly throughout the book. She rises to meet challenge after challenge as the war destroys the world she was born into as a daughter of the South. Tara made her charming, but the war made her Scarlett O'Hara.

The cynicism of Rhett Butler is still breathtaking and his black-hearted, impudent humor resonates throughout the book. He serves as the clarifying eye in the midst of so much high-toned discussion of the cause and the Southern way of life. His is the first sounding of the New South, rising out of the chaos left in the passing of the old order. Yet in the arc of his character, it is Rhett and Rhett alone who seems to change most dramatically. He, who never lets an opportunity pass to mock the pieties and abstractions of Southern patriotism, joins the Confederate Army only when its defeat is certain. Rhett Butler, who profited greatly while blockade running, food speculating, and bankrolling prostitutes, turns out to be the softest of fathers, the most self-sacrificing of friends, the most flamboyant and ardent of lovers; yet it is his wounded masculinity that reveals the secret toll the war took on the South. His one great flaw was making the terrible and exhilarating mistake of falling in love with Scarlett O'Hara.

Both Scarlett and Rhett are perfect repre-

sentatives of the type of Southerner who pros-
pered amid the ruins of a conquered nation.
They both collaborated with the occupying
army, both survived by embracing pragma-
tism and eschewing honor. Rhett and Scarlett are the two characters who let you know
what the South will become. Ashley Wilkes
and Melanie Hamilton Wilkes let you know
what the South was and will never be again.
The practicality of both Rhett and Scarlett
make them the spiritual parents of Atlanta.
Born of fire, Atlanta was the first Southern
city to fall in love with the party of hustle and
progress. The burning of Atlanta increased
the city's lack of roots and made it even more
like Dayton than Charleston. Rhett and Scarlett were masterful at cutting deals and playing the percentages and not looking back,
and they bequeathed these gifts to the reborn
city itself.

I owe a personal debt to this novel that I
find almost beyond reckoning. I became a
novelist because of **Gone with the Wind,**
or more precisely, my mother raised me up
to be a "Southern" novelist, with a strong
emphasis on the word "Southern," because
Gone with the Wind set my mother's imagination ablaze when she was a young girl in
Atlanta, and it was the one fire of her bruised,
fragmented youth that never went out. I still

wonder how my relationship with the language might be different had she spoon-fed me Faulkner or Proust or Joyce, but my mother was a country girl new to the city, one generation removed from the harsh reality of subsistence farming, and her passion for reading received its shaping thrust when **Gone with the Wind** moved its heavy artillery into Atlanta to fight its rearguard action against the judgment of history itself.

When my mother described the reaction of the city to the publication of this book, it was the first time I knew that literature had the power to change the world. It certainly changed my mother and the life she was meant to lead. She read the novel aloud to me when I was five years old, and it is from this introductory reading that I absorbed my first lessons in the authority of fiction. There is not a sentence in this book unfamiliar to me since my mother made a fetish of rereading it each year. The lines of **Gone with the Wind** remain illustrated in gold leaf in whatever disfigured Book of Kells I carry around with me from my childhood. I can close my eyes today and still hear my mother's recitation of it in the same reverential voice she used when she read to me from the story of Genesis.

When she drove me to Sacred Heart School

and we moved south along Peachtree Street, she could point out areas where the two armies of the Americas clashed. She would take me to the spot outside the Loew's Grand Theatre and show me where she was standing in the crowd on the night that the movie premiered in Atlanta and she saw Clark Gable and Vivien Leigh and Margaret Mitchell enter the theater to great applause. Though she could not afford a ticket, she thought she owed the book the courtesy of standing among the crowd that night. Together, we visited the grave of Margaret Mitchell at Oakland Cemetery, and Mom would say a decade of the rosary over her tombstone, then remark proudly that the novelist had been a Roman Catholic of Irish descent. On weekends, she would drive me to Stone Mountain to view the half-finished effigies of Southern generals on horseback carved into the center of that massive granite outcropping, then off to Kennesaw Mountain and Peachtree Creek, where she taught me the battle of Atlanta according to the gospel of Margaret Mitchell. My mother, during these visitations, taught me to hate William Tecumseh Sherman with my body and soul, and I did so with all the strength I could bring to the task of malice. He was the Northern general, presented as the embodiment of evil, who had burned the pretty city where I was born. Mom would drive me near the spot where Margaret Mitchell was struck down by a taxicab in 1949 and look toward the skyline at Five Points, saying, "Can you imagine how beautiful Atlanta would be if Sherman had never been born?"

But the story of this novel and my mother goes deeper than mere literary rapport. I think that my mother, Frances Dorothy Peek, known to all as Peg, modeled her whole life on that of Scarlett O'Hara. I think that fiction itself became such a comfortable country for me because Mom treated the book as though it were a manual of etiquette whose dramatis personae she presented as blood relations and kissing cousins rather than as creations of one artist's imagination. She could set our whole world against this fictional backdrop with alarming ease. Mom, the willful, emotional beauty with just the right touch of treachery and flirtation, was Miss Scarlett herself. Dad, the Marine Corps fighter pilot, flying off the deck of his aircraft carrier, dropping napalm on the enemy North Koreans an entire world away, played the role of the flashy, contemptuous Rhett Butler. Aunt Helen was the spitting image of Melanie Wilkes, Mom would inform me as she prepared our evening meal, and Aunt Evelyn acted just like Suellen. Uncle James could play the walk-on part for Charles Hamilton, and Uncle Russ the stand-in for Frank Kennedy. Mom could align our small universe with that of **Gone with the Wind** while she stirred the creamed corn. Once she had read the novel, it lived inside her the rest of her life, like a bright lamp she could always trust in the darkness.

Even my young and tenuous manhood was informed by lessons of instruction from her interpretation of the novel, which she would fight about with my father. "No matter what girls say," Mom would say, "they'd much rather marry a man like Ashley Wilkes than Rhett Butler."

"I hate Ashley Wilkes," Dad would say. Literary criticism was not an art form conducted at a high level in my family, and I still do not believe my father ever read my mother's sacred text. "That guy's a pansy if I've ever seen one. Of course, Rhett Butler's a pansy compared to me." Mom would turn to me, sniff, and say, "Your father's from Chicago. He doesn't even know what we're talking about."

Gone with the Wind presented my mother and people like her with a new sense of themselves. She hailed the book as the greatest book ever written or that ever would be written, a nonpareil that restored the South's sense of honor to itself after the unimaginable horrors of war and occupation. I have come across legions of critics who deplored my mother's taste in fiction, but this was my mother and I was heir to that taste, for better or worse. Mom's hurt childhood had damaged something irreparable in her sense of self, and I think she won it back by her obsessive identification with Scarlett O'Hara. My mother's family suffered grievously during the Depression, but Scarlett taught that one could be hungry and despairing, but not broken and not without resources, spiritual in nature, that precluded one from surrendering without a fight. When Scarlett swears to God after rooting around for that radish in the undone garden of Tara that she will never go hungry again, she was giving voice to every American who had suffered want and fear during the Hoover years. It was this same Scarlett who gave Southern women like my mother new insights into the secrecies and potentials of womanhood itself, not always apparent in that region of the country where the progress of women moves most slowly. **Gone with the Wind** tells the whole story of a lost society through the eyes of a single woman, and that woman proves match enough for a world at war, an army of occupation, and every man who enters those sugared realms of her attraction. Rarely has a heroine so immoral or unscrupulous as Scarlett O'Hara held the deed to center stage during the course of such a long novel.

Whenever the movie version was released again by MGM, Mom would march all her children to the local theater with a sense of religious anticipation. I remember that feeling of participating in some rite of sacred mystery when the movie began and my mother let herself be taken once again by this singular, canonical moment in Southern mythmaking. She would hum along when the theme from Tara began playing and she would weep at all the right places. I would observe her watching her heroine, Scarlett O'Hara, mouthing the words as Scarlett spoke them to Ashley, to Rhett, to Melanie, to the Yankee interloper who desecrated the sanctuary of Tara, and I would be thinking what I think now—that my mother was as pretty as Scarlett O'Hara; that she had modeled herself on this fictional creation and had done so as an act of sheer will and homage. I would wonder if anyone else in the theater could see what was so obvious to me—that this movie belonged to my mother; that it was the site of her own invention of herself, the place where she came to revive her own deepest dream of her lost girlhood. The movie version of **Gone with the Wind,** like the book, was a house of worship my mother retired to so she could experience again the spiritual refreshment of art.

Yet it is as a work of art that **Gone with the Wind** has been most suspect. From the beginning, the book has endured the incoming fire of some of the nation's best critics. It is a book of Dickensian power, written after the dawn of the age of Joyce's **Ulysses**. Its vigorous defense of the Confederacy was published three years before the German panzer divisions rolled across the borders of Poland. In the structure of Margaret Mitchell's perfect society, slavery was an essential part of the unity and harmony of Southern life before Fort Sumter. No black man or woman can read this book and be sorry that this particular wind has gone. The Ku Klux Klan plays the same romanticized role it had in **The Birth of a Nation** and appears to be a benign combination of the Elks Club and a men's equestrian society. Critics took the novel apart from the beginning, then watched as it proceeded to become the best-selling book in American history. Its flaws may have doomed a lesser book, but this one rode out into literary history with Rhett and Scarlett in complete command of the carriage.

Literature often has a soft spot for the lost cause. Defeat lends an air of tragedy and nostalgia that the victors find unnecessary. But history will forgive almost anything, except being outwritten. None can explain the devotion that **Gone with the Wind** has inspired from one generation to another, but one cannot let this ardor go unremarked upon either. Because its readers have held it in such high esteem, it has cheapened the book's reputation as a work of art. Democracy works because of the will of the people, but it has the opposite effect when scholars begin to call out those books that make up the canon of our nation's literature. **Gone with the Wind** has outlived a legion of critics and will bury another whole set of them after this century closes.

The novel works because it possesses the inexpressible magic where the art of pure storytelling rises above its ancient use and succeeds in explaining to a whole nation how it came to be this way. There has never been a reader or a writer who could figure out why this happens to only a very few books. It involves all the eerie mysteries of enchantment itself, the untouchable wizardry that occurs when a story, in all its fragile elegance, speaks to the times in a clear, original voice and answers some strange hungers and demands of the zeitgeist. I know of no other thousand-page book that grants such pleasure. The characters are wonderful, and the story moves with bright, inexorable power.

The book allows you to lose yourself in the glorious pleasures of reading itself, when all five senses ignite in the sheer happiness of narrative. The Civil War and its aftermath may not have felt like this at all, but it sure seems that way when one gets carried away in the irresistible tumult and surge of **Gone with the Wind**. This book demonstrates again and again that there is no passion more rewarding than reading itself, that it remains the best way to dream and to feel the sheer carnal joy of being fully and openly alive.

Gone with the Wind has many flaws, but it cannot, even now, be easily put down. It still glows and quivers with life. American letters will always be tiptoeing nervously around that room where Scarlett O'Hara dresses for the party at Twelve Oaks as the War Between the States begins to inch its way toward Tara.

CHAPTER THREE

THE TEACHER

My father confused me about what it meant to become a man. From an early age, I knew I didn't want to be anything like the man he was. If I'd become a wife- or child beater, it would be only a matter of time before I would've severed the carotid artery that carried blood into the troubled countryside of my brain. Among his fellow marines, Donald Conroy's horrible taste proved unerring, and he attracted a string of oddball friends who should've been eligible for any catch-and-release program. For the most part, they were third-rate men who spread rich marmalades of loathing over their own wives and children. I was on a lifelong search for a different kind of man. I wanted to attach my own moon of solitude to the strong attraction of a good man's gravitational pull. I found that man by luck when I walked into Gene Norris's English class in 1961. Though Gene couldn't have survived a fistfight with any of the marines I had met, I knew I was in the presence of the exceptional and scrupulous man I'd been searching for my whole life. The certainty of his gentleness was like a clear shot of sunshine to me. I had met a great man, at last.

In my career, I've written enough about Gene Norris's seminal role in my life to warrant Gene's own demurral and note of complaint. Even from his hospital bed, he would scold me for my constant advocacy of him as the grand irreplaceable lodestar of my boyhood. Gene would remind me that I had other fine teachers at Beaufort High School and that I should concentrate on celebrating them instead of chattering on and on about his influence. I replied that all teachers could sustain themselves if they read about the English teacher who found a profoundly shy and battered young man and changed the course of his life with the extravagant passion he brought to his classroom. I tried to visit Gene every time he went to the hospital in Columbia to receive chemotherapy treatment for his leukemia, and he and I would talk for hours. I'd depart when he entered into a co-malike sleep that would sometimes leave him trembling with its fierce possession. On occasion he would lash out and cuss me for wasting time with him when I could be working on my novel. Once he screamed at me when he heard I was writing an article about him for **House Beautiful**.

"Creature, do I look like a house to you?" Gene asked.

"Yeah, you do, Gene. You look like an outhouse."

"Do I look beautiful to you, Irish Gypsy?" he yelled, drawing the attention of a pretty nurse.

"Anything wrong, Mr. Norris?" she inquired.

"Damn right," Gene said. "Throw this scoundrel out with the morning trash. He's a constant irritant and lowbrow to boot. He was born nothing. His family is nothing. He's made a mess of his entire adult life. Call your largest orderly and have him thrown down the hospital steps on his ear."

"Mr. Norris and I've been lovers for over twenty years," I said to the nurse.

"I'll be dammed if that's so. Scram, young lady. There's no telling what filth will spew from his treacherous lips. He's capable of saying anything. There's no muzzle or governor on his gas pedal to stop him or even slow him down. His humbuggery knows no limits."

"Humbuggery?" I repeated. "I feel like I'm living in London. I'm visiting Charles Dickens."

"You're nothing but a knave and a flibbertigibbet," Gene said, his eyes fixed on the nurse's reaction.

"You need anything, Mr. Norris?" the nurse asked.

"Another visitor. Remove this scoundrel when you go," he demanded. "Or you'll be checking the want ads tomorrow morning. This is no idle threat, Nurse."

"Thanks for what you're doing for Mr. Norris," I said to the nurse. "All the nurses have been wonderful."

"We're all in love with Mr. Norris," she said as she shut the door.

"Hogwash. Just pure hogwash," Gene said after she left; then he turned to me to say, "I think we put on a pretty good show. The nurses love it when we talk nonsense to each other. They love the piffle, the endless banter."

"I need to be going, Gene."

"What do you have better to do than visit your old English teacher?"

"Gotta get back to watch the fender on my Buick rust," I said. "Then I got to buy work gloves at Belk's."

"Don't go yet. Please. Tell me a story, one about us. Tell what it meant. How on earth did it happen? The story, Pat—tell it to me."

Gene extended his left hand, and I took it

with both hands and held it as I told him of the fifteen-year-old boy who did not know the name of another student at Beaufort High School. That boy had been taught by nuns and priests his whole life, and like most Catholic school veterans, he could diagram complicated English sentences as gracefully as a fly fisherman casting toward a still pool in a mountain stream.

The boy watched the teacher enter his class, surprised when the teacher noticed him standing beside his desk waiting for the teacher to lead the class in a prayer, then granting permission for the class to take their seats. The teacher walked down the aisle and pushed the boy into his seat and said, "Just sit, boy. You must be some kind of fool or something."

I was not a fool, Gene Norris, but one of the ways I found that out was by attaching my fate to the unprepossessing man who began by telling his students what he expected us to learn over the course of a year, the number of books he required us to read, and the quality of essays we would write. With English department funds, he had gotten each of us a subscription to **The Atlantic Monthly** and **Harper's Magazine**. He expected us to have an intimate knowledge of current affairs and required that we become familiar with the

New York Times. Segregation was still the law of the land in South Carolina. We were an all-white school with all-white teachers, but the world was changing at a bewildering pace around us, and we needed to make ourselves knowledgeable and informed as we ripened into students who would one day offer leadership to the communities we lived in. His eloquence was so understated that it was almost unnoticeable. He displayed a complete assurance in the composure and ease he brought to the art of teaching. At the end of the first day, I was impressed with the man; by the end of the first week, I was in love with him.

"There you go again," Gene said when I paused in telling the story. "Always gilding the lily. Always exaggerating. From the very start, I tried to get you to tone it down, reel it in. Pull it back. But you were incapable of listening to a simple instruction. Oh, no, you did it your way, and no one else's way counted for a thing."

"Where did I exaggerate, Gene?"

"The love part. You talk about love like it's for sale on the cheap. A week. You loved me after a week. What bull-oney. What shoddy thinking."

"It wasn't thinking. It was feeling."

"You've already ruined the story," he snapped. "I won't listen to another word."

"Let me defend myself. Over forty years have passed since I was your English student. Who is the man holding your hand in a Columbia hospital talking about a class so few remember? That whole class fell in love with you that year. I was a witness to it all. I remember everything."

"Go on," he said, relenting.

My first week in his class, Gene Norris played a record at the beginning of the period. It was called "The Death of Manolete," a journalist's awed account of a bull killing a legendary bullfighter during a corrida in Spain. Manolete's footwork was magnetic and flawless and his cape work was a study in perfection as the great-horned beast and the clown-faced man performed a demonic ballet to the joyous applause of the crowds. But on that day, the prodigies of Manolete met the instinctive genius of a bull bred for combat, and the goring was terrible and forgotten by no one in attendance. I told Gene that he made us write an essay about what Manolete must have felt that day, or what the bull felt or what the men and women felt who watched in horror as Manolete was carried out on a stretcher.

"You wrote about how the bull felt," Gene said. "The only one who ever did. That's when I spotted you."

On weekends, as I reminded Gene, he began to invite me to go "rambling" and we'd explore Charleston, Savannah, Bluffton, and Edisto Island. "You introduced me to every antique dealer in the Low Country," I told him, including Mr. Schindler, whom I visited often during my cadet days at The Citadel. He always called me "the professor's boy," and his refinement and courtesy seemed to be native shrubs of Charleston itself. Those trips sealed Gene's and my friendship forever and opened up a world I never imagined existed. "Then basketball season started," I continued, "and you always drove part of the team in your car on road trips. I always sat next to you in the front seat. You made those trips wonderful adventures for all of us."

"After the first game I teased you about being a star," Gene said. "You blushed down to your toes. I said, 'Lawdy, Lawdy, imagine little ol' Gene Norris teaching a real star in my classroom. Praise the Lord, I'm not worthy of such an honor.'"

"You were a pain in the ass."

"But I didn't teach astronomy," he continued, ignoring me. "I knew nothing about the heavenly bodies. What was I supposed to do with an actual star sitting in the front row of my classes? Buy a telescope? Read up on Galileo?"

In December 1961, Gene accompanied the basketball team on its annual road trip to Myrtle Beach. I stayed with the Diminich family, who owned an Italian restaurant named Roma, where I tasted both garlic and olive oil for the first time in my life. Gene enjoyed the shrimp scampi so much that he served it at dinner parties for the rest of his life. Gene picked me up after I attended Mass with the Diminich family on Sunday morning and drove me to the Chesterfield Inn for lunch. Myrtle Beach is a shoddy, unplanned city that looks like it killed all its architects before it approved a master plan for its construction. But Gene and his family had stayed at the elegant Chesterfield Inn for as long as he could remember. Guests ate on real china and Gene had to instruct me on which utensil to use as impeccably dressed waiters served the meal. He taught me how to unfold my napkin and spread it on my lap. The crowd was hushed and appreciative as they conversed in murmurous tones at the tables around us. According to Mr. Norris, the Chesterfield reminded him of an inn in London where he had stayed for two weeks.

"Ah, England. Ah, England. There's such

beauty there, Pat. Beauty beyond my powers to describe. How is your Dover sole?"

"It's great, Mr. Norris. I love Dover sole."

"That's good to know. But you aren't eating Dover sole, boy. That's a South Carolina flounder with a gussied-up, royal name."

"The biscuits sure are good," I said.

"When you are enjoying a superb cuisine in a marvelous restaurant like this one, elevate your language, Pat. Make your conversation fresh and exciting. Speak about the noble art of bread making. These biscuits are the grand result of hundreds of years of trial and error. At the table, bring up ideas, talk philosophy. To be boring is not just a sin; it's a crime."

"These biscuits sure are good, Mr. Norris," I said, and he laughed with pleasure.

"Scalawag. What am I going to do about you, scalawag?"

The rest of the team had left early for Beaufort, and Mr. Norris drove down Highway 17 at a leisurely pace, taking time to show me the antebellum homes in the small coastal town of Georgetown and lamenting the fact that all the antique stores were closed up on the Sabbath. Passing by the Sunset Lodge, he commented dryly that it was the largest whorehouse in South Carolina and one of its most popular tourist destinations. Wide-eyed with curiosity, I stared at the unimpressive motor lodge, half expecting volcanic smoke to rise out of the provenance of such corruption. I stared hard at those contaminated grounds hoping that scantily clad beauties with For Sale signs hanging from their necks would prance into view.

"This place even smells funny," I said to Mr. Norris.

"You ain't smelling no women, son," he said. "That's the paper mill we just passed in Georgetown."

A mist was rising off the Santee River as we crossed the bridge heading toward Charleston. Several times, Gene had checked his wristwatch and now he took a hard right down an uninhabited country road that ran parallel to the Santee itself. For several miles we rode in silence until he turned into a road at a small sign that said, HAMPTON PLANTATION, 1735.

Driving up in front of the many-columned plantation house, Gene ordered me to comb my hair and straighten myself up. He insisted that I put my thoughts in shipshape order and hold up my end of the conversation with both wit and decorum. He had arranged for me to meet the most famous writer in South Carolina, and he demanded that I be cordial, inquisitive, and respectful. A tall, distinguished man with impeccable manners and a courtly demeanor greeted us at the front door.

"Hello, Mr. Norris," he said. "It's a pleasure to see you again. Is this the young man you spoke so highly of?"

"It certainly is. The young man's name is Pat Conroy. This is the poet laureate of South Carolina, Mr. Archibald Rutledge."

"It's an honor to meet you, sir." I said it in a state of shock that I was meeting a writer for the first time in my life.

"Mr. Norris tells me that you show a rare aptitude in your work. Do you prefer poetry or prose?"

"I'd like to be a poet, sir," I said. Mr. Rutledge was straight backed and well groomed and as crisp as a stalk of celery. He wore leather patches at the elbows of his sports coat and demonstrated an innate courtliness that I couldn't imitate in a hundred years. He introduced us to his wife, Alice Rutledge; then he led me into his study, where he composed his poetry and kept his books. He had stocked his shelves with leather-bound sets and the room smelled of tobacco smoke and tannery hides. His voice was calm, modulated, and unrushed. Though his inflections were Southern, they were highborn and polished beneath the fretwork of manor houses.

Lifting a piece of paper from his desk, he read a new poem he had written out in a handwriting that looked to me like jasmine weaving through a trellis. He read two rhyming stanzas to me, then said, "How do you like them, Mr. Conroy?"

"I wish I'd written them, sir," I said.

"A high compliment, young man," Archibald Rutledge said. "How would you improve them?"

"I don't think I could."

"Writing can always be improved," he told me. "Please help me improve this first draft."

"A stronger rhyme at the end of the first stanza," I suggested.

"A fair observation," he said, studying his poem in embryo. "I'll take your advice into consideration."

Then Archibald Rutledge took me on a leisurely tour of his home, pointing out felicities of style and architectural ornament that he found significant. We toured the gardens and he walked me down a pathway to the forest that crowded up to the edge of the plantation. He knelt down to show me where a white-tailed buck had sharpened his antlers against a cypress tree before the beginning of mating season. He suggested that I make the close observation of nature part of my life's work and that I learn the actual names of things, saying that specifics always proved fruitful to the validity of any narrative.

"A Cherokee rose, not just a rose. A swallowtail butterfly, not just a butterfly. That kind of thing," he said. "Get the details right. Always the details."

I followed him down another path, which led to the edge of the marsh and the great, vast reaches of the Santee River. He told me that his ancestors had been entertaining Francis Marion, the famous Swamp Fox whose tactics in guerrilla warfare had flummoxed the English troops, when a patrol of British cavalry arrived at the plantation's front entrance. The Swamp Fox had sprinted out the back door and made his escape by swimming the Santee River, then hiding in the attic of another plantation upriver. Hampton Plantation had played a small but necessary role in the revolution that cleansed the country of British rule. With a sweeping gesture of his hand, he informed me that he and his wife did not really own Hampton Plantation, but they were lucky enough to walk the world as "visitors" to such a distinguished home place.

"We are visitors in every house we ever enter, Mr. Conroy," he said. "It's important that you remember that when you begin to write. And don't forget you were once a visitor to Hampton Plantation, just as I am."

"I'll never forget it, sir," I said.

On our drive back through Charleston, Gene asked me how I liked Archibald Rutledge. I admitted that I was unprepared to meet such an important man and could hardly believe that he had spent so much time with me and seemed so unhurried as he answered my foolish, boyish questions. I told Gene that Archibald Rutledge had told me about the definitive value of details; then I described the path where Francis Marion had escaped the British cavalry patrol. I spoke of camellia bushes ten feet high and the color of ink Mr. Rutledge used to write his poems and that his ancestors had built the plantation in 1735.

"You didn't learn the most important thing," Gene said. "I thought there was more to you. Substance, that kind of thing. I gave you credit for having a substance you don't."

"What're you talking about?"

"Here's what you should've learned, but you didn't. Now you know how to treat a young boy or girl who wants to be a writer. If, by a miracle, you become a writer, Archibald Rutledge just showed you how a famous writer treats a no-account sixteen-year-old boy who's got the same dreams he did as a kid."

"If I ever get to be a writer, Mr. Norris, I'll be nice to every kid I meet. That's a promise."

It was a throwaway pledge I made in the giddiness of having just met a working poet for the first time, but Gene Norris would never let me forget it. Over the years, when a resourceful high school student was writing a report on one of my books, Mr. Norris became the primary source for getting in touch with me. He threw that day at Hampton Plantation and my visit with Archibald Rutledge in my face for the rest of his life.

"Norris, Norris, please listen to me," I would whine. "I've got books to write. I've got kids in college. When will my debt to you be stamped 'paid in full'?"

"This little girl from Laurens is seventeen, a lovely, darling girl, bright as a penny made in Denver. She's doing a paper on **The Prince of Tides**. I told her you'd call her tomorrow night."

"You can't do this, Gene. You just can't do it."

"I seem to remember a sixteen-year-old boy. He was in my class over thirty years ago. He sure would've liked to talk to a real writer. It seems I took him to meet a Mr. Archibald Rutledge, who was sure nice to that snot-nosed boy."

"What's the damn telephone number, Norris?"

So, over the years, I would call the girl in

Laurens or the sweetheart of a boy from Prosperity or the cheerleader from Spartanburg or the drum major from Conway. South Carolina is a state of contained, unshared intimacies. It is a state of crosscurrents, passwords, secret handshakes, but it rewards the lifelong curiosity of both natives and strangers alike. When I called an honor student in Orangeburg, I would touch down into the lives of fifty families who loved that child and every English class in that high school. I never called a kid who found me through the good offices of Gene Norris who was not scrupulously prepared, inquisitive, and nimble-footed. Their questions were so refined that I couldn't get off the phone in less than an hour. Some of them confessed that my great English teacher had spent several phone calls making sure that they were well equipped for their interviews with me. All of them were appreciative and grateful for my time, but I could tell that every one of them was nuts over Gene Norris.

After Christmas of my junior year, Gene put me in charge of selling paperback books from display racks on the right side of his desk. The bookstore in town sold mostly office supplies, so Gene found it easier to order books wholesale from publishing companies to make sure that his students had access to the great literature of our times. I opened the store at lunchtime and sold books to any student who wanted to buy them. I gained a reputation among the jocks for knowing the shortest works of literature ever written by accomplished writers. I had fullbacks reading Steinbeck's **Of Mice and Men,** the offensive line reading Orwell's **Animal Farm,** and the whole track team dashing through Hemingway's **Old Man and the Sea**. But the high school had a passel of bright, ambitious kids who would one day walk the halls of Harvard, Princeton, Stanford, and other schools of that reputation. I sold two **Moby Dick**s, a handful of **Scarlet Letter**s, a bunch of **Great Gatsby**s with a couple of Cather's **Death Comes for the Archbishop**s, and Booker T. Washington's **Up from Slavery**.

But the most popular book I sold that season could not be displayed or sold without due diligence or Mr. Norris's personal permission. Gene Norris had championed **The Catcher in the Rye** since its publication, but he had a heartfelt talk with every student who bought it and explained its incendiary and controversial reputation. Because it was sold as contraband and because there is no taste so ambrosial as forbidden fruit, **The Catcher in the Rye** was the runaway best seller during my time as a salesman in Gene Norris's class. The purchase of **The Catcher in the Rye** felt like a revolutionary act during those years of gathering disturbance in the Southern psyche. When I wrote a book report on it, I drew a huge laugh from Mr. Norris by declaring that any high school student who failed to identify with Holden Caulfield was a worthless loser or a pathetic brownnoser. But **Catcher in the Rye** had a way of snake-biting even its most dexterous handlers, and Gene was called before the school board to answer the bitter complaints of parents who thought he was in the business of corrupting the innocence of their children.

When Gene prepared to confront the school board—a test he welcomed—he asked me to write a summation and defense of the novel from a high school student's point of view. I worked on the paper for a week, but lived in fear that I would damage Mr. Norris's reputation if I said what I was really thinking. I wrote something cowardly and milquetoasty, and Gene Norris would have nothing to do with it. Instead of scolding me or holding me up to ridicule, he approached it as a great teacher must and delivered a lesson I would take with me for the rest of my life.

"Pat, you're not saying what's in your heart. You write as though you're afraid of something. But our work here is literature.

Nothing more or less. Literature tells us to be brave. It demands it of us. We are fighting so that Holden Caulfield's voice can be heard. If they silence him who is next? Will it be Hester Prynne or Ishmael or Eugene Gant, your new favorite? You say you wrote this paper, but it's somebody else, somebody you think you're supposed to be. It's not the boy I know you to be."

"I can make it better, Mr. Norris."

"I know you can," he said. "But you need some help from your teacher. Go back and write it. But don't do it the same way. The next time write it like Holden Caulfield would write it. Come out swinging. Do it for Holden. Do it for you and for me."

In a white heat, I wrote my defense of **The Catcher in the Rye** using the wisecracking, disconsolate voice of Holden Caulfield. I wrote it in one fiery take. When Mr. Norris read it the next day, he whistled and laughed and groaned. "You'll get both of us run out of town. We'll be strung up by a posse in the train yards of Yemassee. Boy, this is way too hot to handle. It's perfect. I wouldn't let you change a word of it."

When Gene Norris went before the school board to defend his teaching of **The Catcher in the Rye,** I was in the audience holding tight to my own intemperate apologies for the novel. The world of adults both appalled and intimidated me, but I found myself pacified by the eloquence of my English teacher. He talked about the things literature could do and not do, but he believed that a great book could do whatever it wanted. He reminded the school board that neither the parents who condemned the Salinger book nor any board member had bothered to read it. Great books invited argument and disagreement, but ignorance did not even earn a place at the table when ideas were the subject of dispute. Gene told the group that he would stake his reputation on the integrity of **Catcher in the Rye** as a novel. In his heart, he believed that the portrait of Holden Caulfield was the most authentic rendition of a modern-day teenager in American fiction. If they wanted to ban one of Gene's choices, then the board of education should go ahead and banish all of them, because books existed to force people to examine every facet of their lives and beliefs. Because of the power of its ideas, the Bible was banned in the Soviet Union. There was nothing to fear in **The Catcher in the Rye** except the danger of its being censored by people who hadn't read it. Mr. Norris's passion and his common sense won the hearts of the school board, and Holden Caulfield walked the streets of Beaufort as a free man from that day forward.

When Mr. Norris drove me home that night, I was giddy with a free-flowing sense of triumph. I was also grateful that I'd not been called on to address the school board. The atmosphere seemed inimical to anything a kid might have to say.

"Oh, I'd never have called on you to deliver your paper, scalawag," Gene said.

"Why not?"

"Because they'd have fired me on the spot. Too hot to handle."

"Then why'd you have me write it?" I asked.

"To see what you really thought. You hide everything about yourself. We've got to change that, son."

One Sunday each month, Mr. Norris would pick me up at our family's quarters in base housing and drive me over to St. Helena Island for the community sing at the Penn Center. Quaker activists had formed the Penn School in the middle of the Civil War as a testing ground in teaching the newly freed slaves in what was called the Port Royal Experiment. Always, Gene and I were usually the only white people in the hall where the black islanders would gather to sing the spirituals that fortified and sustained their ancestors during the harrowing time of slavery. Their voices lifted up in the dark melancholy of history, the shine of mahogany blending with the density of wood smoke as the voices discovered a stirring, perfect harmony. I can still sing the words of the first spiritual I ever heard at Penn Center.

The ole sheep done know the road,
The young lambs must find the way.

The singing carried with it an authenticity that seemed beyond criticism to me. Though these were the sons and daughters of slaves, they were keeping alive the songs that kept their ancestors hopeful during the tearful nights of their captivity. I was listening to the heart of Africa beating the dream of liberation on a sea island that had welcomed them in chains. Often, Gene and I would drift across the street to the home of Courtney and Elizabeth Siceloff, the white Quaker couple who ran the center and who knew most of the black leadership in Beaufort years before anyone else did. Besides my mother, Gene Norris was the first white Southerner I knew who was a sworn enemy of segregation and the Jim Crow laws.

One Sunday after the community sing,

a young Martin Luther King Jr. got up to preach a homily, and I heard the most electrifying speaker I had ever listened to. His voice was an instrument of an immense and subtle power. He spoke without notes, his voice both a spillage of honey and a quiet call to arms. Later, I met him at the Siceloffs' house and learned that he, his family, and colleagues often retreated to Penn Center to plan the next phase of the civil rights movement. When a photographer began snapping pictures of the gathering, I kept watching as Mr. Norris went to his knees to tie his shoes. The third time I saw him go down to lace up his troublesome shoe, I bent down and offered to show him how to tie a double knot. He went on tying his shoe as he whispered to me, "If a photograph of me socializing with Dr. King ever gets in the **Beaufort Gazette,** I'll be run out of this town on a rail. Whenever you see that man aiming his camera at me, I'll know my shoes are untied." Later I would watch Dr. King in serious discussion with Gene Norris, and I was one of the few people in Beaufort County to know that a rare friendship had sprung up between them.

Gene Norris didn't just make his students love books; he made us love the entire world. He was the essential man in the lives of a thousand boys and girls who dwelled in

the shadow of his almost unnoticeable greatness. When Mike Sargent's father was killed
in Vietnam, Mike barely knew Mr. Norris
when Gene appeared on his doorstep to offer
his condolences. Mike was a wisecracking, re-
bellious boy, and Gene always reserved a ten-
derhearted place for the bad boys. Although
Mike's relationship with his father had been
violent and bitter, he was devastated by his
father's death and the fact that he could
never be reconciled with him. Gene Norris
did not leave Mike Sargent's house for the
next three days and nights. After the funeral
in the National Cemetery, Gene stepped in
to replace the father forever AWOL in Mike
Sargent's life. Mike would've killed anybody
who harmed Gene, and everyone in Beaufort
knew it. Yet Mike never took a course Mr.
Norris taught.

In 1994, I returned limping to Beaufort
after my train wreck of a second marriage
had fallen apart. In the middle of writing
Beach Music I had collapsed from the inside out and was more suicidal than I'd ever
been. By killing myself, I could rescue my
soul from an agony I could not even touch
in my writing. Gene Norris drove out to my
house on Fripp Island and ordered me to call
my former shrink, Marion O'Neill, who had
relocated her office from Atlanta to Hilton

Head Island. From our first session, Marion thought I was closer to suicide than any patient she had ever treated. It alarmed her, and she and Gene talked on an almost daily basis during those first couple of weeks. Before I left the office on the first day, Marion said, "Pat, you've got to promise me one thing. You've got to promise me that you won't kill yourself. If the author of **Prince of Tides** kills himself while he is my patient, you'll destroy my practice."

I laughed as she knew I would; then Marion commanded me to drive from there to Gene Norris's office. "Sit and talk with Gene for half an hour," she said. "Then drive yourself home. Gene's going to call me after you leave him. You call me when you arrive home."

Each day I would stop by Gene's office at Robert Smalls Junior High, where Gene taught the last fifteen years of his career, helping run the guidance department. I would sit in his office and sometimes weep during our entire time together. He was solicitous and kind. As always, he was Norris-like. As the therapy began to kick in and I started to fight my way back into myself, I got to watch Gene deal with several black students with disciplinary or emotional problems. Not surprisingly, he brought extraordinary gifts to the task at hand. His dedication to his kids and their hero worship of him was a powerful force that rose up among them.

One day, I walked into Gene's office as school was ending, and five black kids impatiently awaited my arrival. Gene motioned for me to follow him; we piled into his Buick and drove to the Highway Department. Gene led his kids into the building and stood in line with them as they received the handbooks they would need to master before they got learner's permits. On the long drive home, Gene made all of his kids study the handbook, promising to take them all back when they had memorized the basics of driving. I was there when all five of them flunked their first exams. Gene went over their incorrect answers and discussed their mistakes and errors with them. I went back a second time and still no one passed. On the third try, one little kid from the community of Sheldon passed the test with a perfect score. A loud cheer went up from our gang as we waited for the kid to get his learner's permit.

When we walked to the car for the long drive home, Gene threw the kid his car keys and said, "You're the driver now, Deontay. According to South Carolina law, you got the stuff to get us home. Prove it."

As I sat in the backseat, with four middle schoolers moaning with envy, Gene carefully guided the young man on back roads that took us to his home without encountering much traffic. When Deontay turned off onto the dirt road where he lived, Gene leaned over and began tooting the horn on his Buick, causing people to come out of a dozen trailers to see what all the commotion was. At the end of the road, Gene spun the steering wheel and turned the car around and ordered the kid to become a little sassy and show-offy when he passed in review in front of his friends and family again. They cheered hard when the newest driver in the neighborhood flashed by them in his teacher's Buick.

When the car stopped and the boy jumped out, he went racing into his mother's arms. Then he turned and cried, "Thank you, Mr. Norris." He grabbed Gene and kissed him. So did the mother. The father. The neighbors who were running up the road to join the impromptu party.

When Gene resumed driving, he said to the other kids, "Same day next week. You kids got to study hard. You just saw what good study habits did for Deontay. We're going to make your families just as proud. Now, study, gentlemen. Study hard. I taught Mr. Conroy this and now I'm teaching it to you. Reading is the key to everything. Right, Tyrone?"

Though I was still shell-shocked and delusional from my latest skirmish with the demons that had trailed me back home, I remember thinking as I stared at Gene Norris, Where do such men come from? Why aren't there more of them?

In 1994, the American Booksellers Association held their annual meeting in Los Angeles, and I was one of the speakers scheduled to address the convention on Saturday. I convinced Gene to let me fly him out to the convention first-class, because I wanted to praise his remarkable gifts as a teacher and tell the story about the part he played in my teenage collision with Thomas Wolfe. It took more than a month of argument to win Gene's approval, because he fought a guerrilla action against every single phase of the trip west. His consent finally came when I promised not to tell the audience that Gene was in attendance, and I had to swear that I would not have him stand up and act like a fool when I mentioned his name. It was only when we took off from the Atlanta airport that I understood Gene had a fear of flying that was immobilizing. I ordered him a martini from the flight attendant, and he said, "I'll be a wino before I set foot in Hollywood."

Gene wandered all through the enormous convention hall accepting every free book and magazine offered by the major and minor publishing companies. To my surprise, he identified himself as my English teacher at several of the booths when he struck up conversations with publicists or sales reps. Someone from Doubleday said Gene wept during my talk about a great English teacher finding me when I was a boy and brand new to a high school in South Carolina.

At a party given at Universal Studios, I watched Gene moving out of the periphery. As I met new members of the Doubleday staff, I lost sight of Gene, who drifted toward the outer perimeters of the party drawn by forces I didn't quite understand. When the party was nearing its completion, I began to search for Gene and was wondering how I would find him in the labyrinthine sets of the studio. I had walked through a New York street scene, passed through a small New England village, then a Western town, when I spotted Gene. He was speaking with a man who was showing him a square in London. The man was clearly enjoying walking Gene though the Hollywood sets where hundreds of movies had been filmed, and I could tell Gene had captivated the stranger with that uniqueness that set Gene apart wherever he went. When Gene caught sight of me, he turned to shake the man's hand, then waved at me and walked through a classical Main Street, USA, façade.

"Remarkable. Just remarkable," Gene said as he joined me and we drifted in step with the crowd moving toward the exit. "I saw where they shot part of **Anna Karenina, Great Expectations,** a dozen Westerns, gangster movies, Southern Gothic novels. . . . It's the damnedest thing I ever saw. That man was a wonderful guide and so knowledgeable. He seemed to know where every film in the world was made."

"You know who that guy is, Gene?" I asked.

"His name's Steven. He says he works out here," Gene said. "He was a generous and very fine man. Very fine indeed."

"That was Steven Spielberg," I told him. I didn't know if Gene Norris had ever watched a movie and do not know to this day.

"Steven knows his business. I predict he'll do well," Gene said.

"Gene, Steven is to the movies what William Faulkner is to books."

"So you've heard of him?"

"Yes, I have."

Over the years I would introduce Gene Norris to dozens of people I met through my writing life. I arranged for him to meet Barbra Streisand, Nick Nolte, Robert Du-

vall, and Blythe Danner, but Gene's character was set in stone years before I met him,
and he remained impervious to any claims
of prestige or celebrity. He was happy in his
own home surrounded by those special an-
tiques and "beauties" that he had collected
over the years in Salvation Army bins and
yard sales. His ex-students came back to his
house by the hundreds and Gene delighted
in the low-maintenance miracle of their return. He knew that they arrived at his doorstep of their own volition, and they came to
thank him for honoring them and breaking
into the immovable storms of aloneness in
the hormonal tempests of their teenage years.
Gene lived for these students who booked
return passages into his life. He would pull
out the yearbooks, and Gene and his visitors
would revisit the lives they lived twenty and
thirty years ago, catching up on the delicious
gossip that was now beginning to sound like
history in the making. When one of his students died, Gene would never forget to cry. If
there is more important work than teaching,
I hope to learn about it before I die.

Gene Norris got me to do more speeches
and fund-raisers than anyone else in my life.
Though I would gripe about them until the
owls flew home and the cock began its morning cry, I would speak pretty much anywhere

Gene asked me to. When he asked me to speak in his hometown for the restoration of the Newberry Opera House, I addressed the crowd before the extensive remodeling began, then returned on that sublime evening when the opera house was restored to its former splendor. I had given the first speech of my life as a writer to a ladies' book club at the opera house in 1972. **The Water Is Wide** was published to a storm of controversy in South Carolina, but the women of Newberry had received me with the utmost courtesy and excitement. I took great pride in the opera house's flawless restoration.

"I used you, Pat," Gene apologized on opening night. "I took advantage of our friendship. I wanted to thank my hometown."

"It was a pleasure and an honor, Gene. I needed to thank Newberry too. And now I have."

"Why would you thank Newberry?"

"It gave me you," I said.

When Gene was diagnosed with leukemia, the Nation of Gene Norris sprang into action. Since we all knew Gene and his countless whims and oddities, we knew he would not accept with much forbearance at all our attempts to help ease his path. Gene grew touchy if someone even mentioned the fact that he had cancer. We learned to avoid the subject unless he brought it up. He would conduct his fight against cancer according to his own unpublished rules. I offered to quit writing when he went into the hospital for chemotherapy and take care of him until he recovered enough to live on his own. He yelled at me when I first suggested this course of action, but Gene was afraid; he was dealing with something uncontrollable for the first time in his life. Soon after he heard the bad news about his health, Gene called me from his parents' house in Newberry and asked me if I would attend a concert at the opera house. I said yes immediately and then Gene told me that Joan Baez was singing that night.

One night after I had gone to a community sing at Penn Center with Gene, he took me to visit his apartment in Beaufort's historic Point afterward. He lived on the second floor of the Christensen house and had a beautiful view of the Beaufort River. I still remember when Gene served me orange juice in a sherry glass and asked me if I'd ever heard of a young folksinger named Joan Baez. He had bought her first Vanguard albums after he heard her singing in a coffeehouse near Harvard Yard several summers before. "Her voice makes me believe in angels. There's a song I think you should hear."

When I heard her voice that night, my heart locked on to it and I felt as if someone were pouring straight silver into my ear. I lost myself to this comely woman whose hair was made from raven wings and midnight as I stared at the jacket cover Mr. Norris had shown me. I've written four or five books listening to Joan Baez's songs over the years. Her voice has always been like a homecoming to me.

As we sat in a box seat at the Newberry Opera House that night, Gene and I were both moved by the queenly presence of Joan Baez when she walked out onto the stage. Her hair was white now and so was ours. When she began to sing, Gene made a strange and unprecedented gesture in our friendship together. He reached over and grasped my hand. He held tightly to my hand for most of the concert and tried to hide the fact that he wept through every song. Something was contained in the mysteries of that night that led to some derangement of Gene's lifelong instincts of forbearance. He had mastered all the styles and habits of the Southern gentleman. But not on this night, not when Joan Baez came to the Newberry Opera House.

When the concert was over and the crowd was heading out into the night, Gene gathered himself together and said that he wanted us to meet Joan Baez, that he wanted that circle completed. We met Joan in her dressing room, and she was as gracious and delightful as I prayed she would be. I told her the story of listening to her voice on that long-ago Southern night when Gene introduced me to a song he thought I needed to hear.

"What song was that?" Joan Baez asked my English teacher. Gene took off his glasses and wiped them clean with his tie, an unconscious gesture I'd watched him do as a kid.

"The song was 'We Shall Overcome,'" he told her. "I think Pat might've been the first white boy in this part of the world to hear it."

"You played that song in the Deep South in the early sixties?" Turning to me, she asked, "Do you know how lucky you are?"

"Yes, I do," I said to Joan Baez while looking at Gene Norris. "I sure as hell do."

When Gene died of leukemia in a Columbia hospital, the world stood still for me. I had spent as much time with him as I could in the last two years of his life. Gene and I had talked every day for the past ten years, no matter where we found ourselves. If I could've been a better friend to Gene Norris I would have done it; and if I failed to, it was a flaw in my character. I don't think I'll ever get over his death and I don't see much reason to try.

After his funeral and burial in Newberry, there was a reception at a pretty restaurant on Main Street, to which I was late after a brief meeting with the other executors of Gene's will. The heat was unbearable and breathing was difficult as I parked the car behind the restaurant. As I walked along a side street, a beautiful young woman called out to me, "Mr. Conroy?"

I turned and this pretty woman kissed me and said, "You don't know me, but we met when I was three years old. You were the May king and my sister was the May queen."

"Ah! Your sister is the lovely Gloria Burns," I said. "But why are you here? Did you know Mr. Norris? You're too young to have been a student of his."

"My first year at Robert Smalls," she said, "I was such a mess. In trouble. Boys. Drugs. That kind of thing. They sent me to Mr. Norris."

"He was good, wasn't he?"

"Mr. Norris told me to come to his office every day at lunch. We could talk and get to know each other. I went there for the next two years. Two years. Yet he didn't even know me."

"You got the best of Gene," I said.

"He saved my life. He literally saved my life."

"Come on in," I said, putting my arm around her. "I'll introduce you to a couple of hundred people who'll tell you the same thing."

"Mr. Norris acted like I was the most important girl in the world," she said.

"You were. That was Gene's secret. All of us were."

In the months leading up to Gene's death, I could not write a word while I was losing the English teacher of my life. When I called Gene to wish him a good night, he always asked me to tell him what I was reading. During the spring and summer before Gene died, I had begun to read the twelve-volume set of Anthony Powell's **A Dance to the Music of Time**. Gene venerated all things English and he liked to end our communications each night with me providing a thumbnail sketch of what I had read the previous day. Throughout the spring and summer, I would keep Gene abreast of all the petty hardships and complaints the narrator records as he makes his way through Eton and then embarks on his upper-middle-class passage into London society in the venomous, suffering England in the feverish days between the wars. He wondered how Powell had discovered the theme of his life's work, and the title of the vast production intrigued him. I told Gene about Powell's coming by accident to a painting by Nicolas Poussin in the Wallace Collection, which is titled **A Dance to the Music of Time**. Though it's a small painting, it carries enormous power and chill factor as four unidentified figures engage in a ritual dance of the seasons or fates or destinies caught up in all the ineffable movements of time.

"Pat, don't you think the passage of time is what all literature is really about? Poems, plays, novels, everything?"

"I think so, Gene."

"Mr. Powell seems to think it's a dance. Do you agree?"

"I wish I'd thought of it before he did."

"You walked into my class in 1961."

"Our dance began."

My summary of those books became a secret language between us and provided a passageway to intimacy that made no mention of his health. It was sublimation and surrender to the efficacy of denial, but it was all very human to me. As I saw it, my job was to follow Gene's wishes and to allow for him to die in his own manner, with strict adherence to the blueprint of his own design. In his dictionary of last days, there were notable blanks in the space that defined the properties of either "cancer" or "leukemia," and those words never passed between us. The Powell novels provided our avenue where we could talk about art and literature and the living of a good life in whatever allotment of time we were given on this earth. When we grew weary of that, he would tell me about the ex-students who called him and the memories each one shared with their former teacher. I waited for his pause, then heard Gene say, "Tell me a story."

I would take Gene back to the England he idealized. The England of fog-banked London streets illuminated by lamplight and the shine of candelabras throwing soft light on shelves of leather-bound books. In the second volume, **A Buyer's Market**, Gene took infinite and voluptuous pleasure in Powell's exacting detailing of set pieces with a large cast of characters—there is a dance at the Huntercombes' and a long dinner that preceded it, a party at Mr. Andriadis's house, and a birthday party for Mr. Deacon. Gene took special pleasure in the decor of rooms, the description of lavish banquets, the elaborate furnishings of upper-class dwelling places as the aristocracy rubbed elbows with the most important artists of the day, and the bizarre

shock waves that could be set off when privi-
leged gentlemen brushed against the lives of
shopgirls armed only with the artillery fire
of their beauty. Like many readers who have
surrendered themselves to the pleasures of
the Powell masterpiece, Gene could not get
enough of that immortal creation of one of
the greatest antiheroes in English letters, the
creepy and power-mad Widmerpool.

Throughout that morbidly hot summer, I
read those twelve volumes and would treasure the moments when I coaxed Gene to
follow me into a world he both coveted and
never knew existed. He sometimes fell asleep
as I was recounting some delicious, gossipy
scene from **Casanova's Chinese Restaurant**
or **Books Do Furnish a Room**.

The month before he died, Gene had a
dream of us on my senior trip to New York.
With infinite pleasure, he recalled my excitement when I looked down at the great city
from the Empire State Building for the first
time. My acceptance of his flippant wager to
reward any boy five bucks if he'd urinate on
the statue of William T. Sherman in Central
Park. His horror when he saw me unzipping
my pants and peeing to the applause of my
classmates.

"I underestimated your attraction to the
most shocking behavior," he said.

"Five bucks looked like a horse blanket to me back then," I explained.

"Then we were riding down Park Avenue, Pat," Gene said. "We were so young then. Even I was young. I was in my early thirties then and thought I'd live forever. Remember where I took you?"

"Yep. You took me to the clock in the Biltmore Hotel. Where Holden Caulfield met Sally Hayes."

"You looked as if I poked you with a cattle prod," Gene said, chuckling at the memory. "I was rewarding you for that essay you wrote to the school board. God, you loved **The Catcher in the Rye!** But you didn't know that was a real clock, or that the Biltmore was a real hotel."

"My teacher was pretty good then."

"So was the student."

A month later, Gene left his Newberry house and entered the Richland County hospital, also for the last time. Again, I called him every night, and though his weakening, unsteady voice alarmed me, he insisted we continue our talks as though nothing had changed. I had reached the final volume of **A Dance to the Music of Time** and I was partial to the luminous title of the last book, **Hearing Secret Harmonies**. I thought that Gene must have been the approximate age

of Anthony Powell when he wrote this elegiac book in his ambitious series. The world
that Powell was born into had transformed
itself into something radical and maybe unspeakable to him. The history we are born
into always seems natural when we're young,
but it seems misshapen and grotesque as the
winter years come upon us. On the last night
we spoke, Gene's voice was unrecognizable
and frantic. Though I tried it was hard to get
him off the phone; he grew angry and I grew
resigned.

"Tell me a story," he commanded, and
I did.

Those were the last words he ever spoke
to me, and they formed an exquisite, unimprovable epitaph for a man whose life was
rich in the guidance of children not his own.
He taught them a language that was fragrant
with beauty, treacherous with loss, comfortable with madness and despair, and a catch-
word for love itself. His students mourned
Gene all over the world, wherever they found
themselves. All were ecstatic to be a part of
the dance.

CHAPTER FOUR

CHARLES DICKENS AND
DAUFUSKIE ISLAND

In 1969, I received a Christmas gift whose staying power is as timeless as water. During the first year of teacher integration in South Carolina, I had volunteered to teach grades five through eight on Daufuskie Island, a remote backwater isle in the coastal lowlands of Beaufort County. For a year, I walked the island and was known as the "white schoolteacher." I taught eighteen black children who were brilliant in the arts of survival, but deficient in academic achievement. I learned that five of them did not know the alphabet, all read below the first-grade level, none knew that the Atlantic Ocean washed up on the shore of their island.

I was in way over my head and lacked all qualifications to teach those kids. Even so, I pulled up a chair and told them not to worry. "I can teach you everything you need to know," I said. "We're going to have a blast."

And a blast we had. They proved to be wonderful students and eager to learn everything I could throw their way. When I

discovered they had never heard of Hallow-
een, I took them trick-or-treating in my town
of Beaufort. After they told me they never
heard of Washington, D.C., I organized a
trip to the nation's capital over the Easter
holidays. Slowly, my students started displaying the confidence that comes from being
smart. Each week, I brought visitors from the
great bright world to them—actors, artists,
musicians—and all came with the fire and
enthusiasm I still associate with the sixties.

One of the great surprises awaiting me on
Daufuskie Island was the presence of two
young white men close to my age. I would
see them walking on the unpaved roads of
the island, and they would refuse to acknowl-
edge me when I waved to them. One day after
the school day ended, the two young men approached me. They asked me if they could
hitch a ride to town in my boat. I refused,
and Jim Ford asked me why.

"Because you don't speak to me," I said.
"You haven't even introduced yourselves.
You pretend I don't exist. So you can swim
to the nearest town."

"We're not allowed to speak to you," Joe
Sanfort said.

"Why not?" I asked.

"Because you're white," he replied.

"You guys ever looked in the mirror?"

"Yes, but you're a **Southern** white man," Joe said. "We can only speak to you in emergencies."

Jim Ford opened his address book and pointed to my telephone number in Beaufort. It was listed under "White Schoolteacher."

The islanders called Jim Ford and Joe Sanfort "the California boys." They were part of a sociology program at the University of California in Santa Cruz. Each quarter, two young men came to Daufuskie to perform fieldwork and interact with the isolated Gullah people. The school authorities banned them from the schoolhouse and tried to keep them away from the children as much as possible.

I took Jim and Joe to Beaufort that weekend, and for most of the weekends to follow. The great loneliness of the island weighed heavily on their spirits, and we struck up a friendship. In the late fall, they asked me to help them put on a community play for the Christmas season. They had chosen an adaptation of Charles Dickens's classic **A Christmas Carol**. One rainy day, I read the entire play to the kids. I've always been a melodramatic, over-the-top reader, and Dickens can be counted on to bring out my worst rendering. When the ghosts made their mordant appearance in that rain-haunted classroom, they scared the daylights out of my eighteen students. Though Dickens was new to those island kids, ghosts were as common as sea oats or beggar's lice, a part of their cultural vernacular. When I left them for the Christmas break, I was confident that the kids knew their parts and that the show would be a good one.

On December 22, I received a desperate phone call from the California boys begging me to return to the island. To call me, Jim and Joe had caught a ride to nearby Bluffton with a fisherman. They were in a panic. Their choice to play the role of Scrooge had always been the demure and ladylike Sarah Jenkins, the beloved midwife who had been present during the delivery of almost all the island residents. During the course of several long rehearsals, it became clear that Aunt Sarah could not read and had been too embarrassed to admit it to anyone. They told me Aunt Sarah suggested I take her place, and they begged me to come.

So go I did. In a candlelit church built on a foundation of tree stumps, its eaves papered with translucent wasps' nests, I stormed about on a makeshift stage, my students around me, full of Dickensian phrases uttered in the purest of Gullah accents. The whole island was there. Though the production was

unimaginably bad, I could feel the moment
when the power of literature took hold, when
the city of London came alive on a Carolina
sea island, and a man in the middle of living
a miserly life reaches out and grabs the only
chance for redemption he has. My children,
my students, were well prepared and beautiful to behold. I strutted ham-fisted and bom-
bastic from one side of the stage to the other.
I scared the little children, caused the fathers
to howl with laughter and the mothers to tell
me I should get a job acting on the soaps. The
Christmas play would change my life among
the island community. The black parents admitted that they had worried about the kind
of white man a mean-spirited South would
send to their island. Because I had crossed a
wild river on a forbidding day for the sake of
my students, they allowed me into the main-
stream of their lives.

The following September I was fired, and
Daufuskie Island was the last place I ever
taught. Each Christmas since then, I watch
the film **A Christmas Carol**. In my imagination, I see my students approaching me
as ghosts who would show me the way to
change my life. I find myself on a river in
the Low Country, going back to an island I
did not recognize as my destiny. And I see

myself returning to the only stage role I ever performed, and to the last children I would ever teach. Those children left me with an inviolate gift, a ghost of Christmas past that burns like the North Star in remembrance.

CHAPTER FIVE

THE LIBRARIAN

I grew up a word-haunted boy. I felt words inside me and stored them wondrous as pearls. I mouthed them and fingered them and rolled them around my tongue. My mother filled my bedtime hour with poetry that rang like Sanctus bells as she praised the ineffable loveliness of the English language with her Georgia-scented voice. I found that hive of words beautiful beyond all conveyance. They clung to me and blistered my skin and made me happy to be alive in the land of crape myrtle, spot-tailed bass, and eastern diamondbacks. The precise naming of things served as my entryway into art. The whole world could be sounded out. I could arrange each day into a tear sheet of music composed of words as pretty as flutes or the tail feathers of peacocks.

From my earliest memories, I felt impelled to form a unique relationship with the English language. I used words to fashion a world that made sense to me. Because we seemed to move every year, I lacked the childhood friends who would offer that invaluable commentary on the progress I was making while drifting through the sun-shot days as a fighter pilot's son. The South gave me stories; the Marine Corps provided me with the fly-over of squadrons; and the Roman Catholic Church offered me a language whose comfort zone included both sweetness and majesty. The Mass lined my Sundays with the underground rhythms of the early Christians who had chosen to adore the flogged, broken Christ. I studied to become an altar boy because I wanted a speaking part in that drama when the murder of Christ transformed itself into the deathlessness of God carried aloft by immensity of faith. Father James Howard instructed me in the Latin prayers and I served my first Mass in the fourth grade at the Annunciation church outside the gates of Cherry Point. When the priest said the words: **"Introibo ad altare Dei:** I will go to the altar of God," I replied by rote, **"Ad Deum, qui laetificat juventutem meam:** To God, the joy of my youth." The goose bumps spread down the keyboard of my spine and I was as caught up with the artfulness and glory of the Mass as was any altar boy who ever wore a surplice and cassock.

Over the years, my church gave me passage into a menagerie of exotic words unknown in the South: "introit," "offertory," "liturgy," "movable feast," "the minor elevation," "the lavabo," "the apparition of Lourdes," and hundreds more. Latin deposited the dark minerals of its rhythms on the shelves of my spoken language. You may find the harmonics of the Common of the Mass in every book I've ever written. Because I was raised Roman Catholic, I never feared taking any unchaperoned walks through the fields of language. Words lifted me up and filled me with pleasure. I've never met a word I was afraid of, just ones that left me indifferent or that I knew I wouldn't ever put to use. When reading a book, I'll encounter words that please me, goad me into action, make me want to sing a song. I dislike pretentious words, those highfalutin ones with a trust fund and an Ivy League education. Often they were stillborn in the minds of academics, critics, scientists. They have a tendency to flash their warning lights in the middle of a good sentence. In literary criticism my eye has fallen on such gelatinous piles as "antonomasia," "litotes," or "enallage."

I've no idea what those words mean nor how to pronounce them nor any desire to look them up. But whenever I read I'll encounter forgotten words that come back to me like old friends who've returned from long voyages to bring me news of the world. Often, I'll begin my writing day by reading those words in the notebooks I keep with such haphazard consistency. Though I'm an erratic journal keeper, I admire the art form well enough to wish I'd had the discipline to master that sideshow of the writer's craft. I lose most of the world around me when I fail to record entries in those notebooks that line my shelves.

I could build a castle from the words I steal from books I cherish. Here's a list I culled from a book I read long ago—"sanction," "outlaw," "suburbia," "lamentations," "corolla," "debris," and "periodic table." I can shake that fistful of words and jump-start a sentence that could send me on my way toward a new book. But if I go forward a single page I can listen to a different reading self who cherry-picked words from another book and recorded "atlas," "villainy," "candelabra," "tango." Each file of words seems outfitted for a different story or novel. I hunt down words that have my initials branded on their flanks. If I take the time to write one down I want to get it right every time I form a sentence. I've known dozens of writers who fear the pitfalls and fastnesses of the language they write in and the glossy mess of the humanity they describe. Yes, humanity is a mess and it takes the immensity of a coiled and supple language to do it justice. Writing is the only way I have to explain my own life to myself. I've amassed a stockpile of books in vaults and storage bins in attics and un-finished basements and tortoiseshell-colored boxes that I raid with willful abandon when I try to fix a sentence on a page. Words call out my name when I need them to make some-thing worthy out of language.

Whenever I sit to write, I never allow my-self the benefit of a Sabbath or day off; nor do I give myself time off for good behavior. Good writing is one of the forms that hard labor takes. It is neither roadhouse nor weigh station, but much more like some unname-able station of the cross. It is taking the noth-ingness of air and turning it into a pleasure palace built on a foundation of words. From the time I could talk I took an immense plea-sure in running down words, shagging them like fly balls in some spacious field. Though I failed to notice it at the time, my childhood was a long, patient apprenticeship of finding my comfort zone in the ocean of words that rushed through me each day. I was drifting toward novels that would one day capture me with the unanswerable power of their rawness, and the sheer need to be told.

The veneration of books carries its own

rewards. When I was seven years old, I was picking through the refuse and castaways in a Cherry Point Dumpster the day after Christmas. Digging through piles of garbage, I came to a heavy box that was bound tightly with cord and tape. The weight of the box was so great that I came close to abandoning the project; then a friend named Gary Snyder came along to lend a hand. Gary was a sweet, wiry kid whose father's fighter plane would crash while on maneuvers near Camp Lejeune. Though it was a struggle, Gary and I lifted the box up out of the Dumpster and heard it fall heavily to the ground. I remember Gary's audible disappointment and my pleasure when we discovered a box full of books. Since Gary had fantasized a chest of doubloons, he wandered away as I inspected a handsome set of the complete works of William Makepeace Thackeray. Of course, I didn't have a clue about Thackeray's identity, but the set was well made and distinguished-looking and there was a silhouette of the author's face embossed on the spine of each book. Two by two, I marched them up to our apartment in "A" building and felt amply rewarded when my mother squealed with pleasure. It was the first set of books Mom had ever owned, and though I'm not certain that she had ever heard of Thackeray, I know for a fact that she devoured his work in the next year of her life. After Scarlett O'Hara, Becky Sharp began to inch her way up the scale of formidable women who made up a glittery all-star team of crinolines and estrogen in Peg Conroy's fictional world. Mom thought the fluttering eyelash and the well-turned ankle could overthrow a kingdom ruled by the brute tyranny of any lawless male. A woman disguised the presence of her own battalions with the timely smile or the modest display of décolletage. In literature, Mom always hungered for the Guineveres who shook the fate of empires out of wantonness or even carelessness. I grew up counseled by Lady Macbeth and Gertrude, advised by Goneril and Regan, and taught to despise the weaklings Ophelia and Cordelia. My mother preferred her heroines to glory in their claws. Once in a forest near Lake Lure, Mom and I watched as two praying mantises mated on an oleander bush and the female began to devour the male's head in the middle of coitus. Though I was embarrassed and horrified to be observing such an intimate act in the presence of my own mother, her reaction to it shocked me even more.

"That's it, girl," Mom said. "That's how to do it!"

The set of Thackeray became emblematic

and definitive to my mother. She would point it out to guests and pepper her conversations with references to **Vanity Fair** and **The History of Henry Esmond**. I was in ninth grade when I read both these novels, and both seemed like old acquaintances. Mom had long since passed into different realms of cultural showing off—Dickens, Jane Austen, and a long stretch she spent riding through the vast, formless steppes during her fruitful engagement with the great Russian writers.

My precocious sister Carol was always in hot pursuit of our mother's reading list. She read **Vanity Fair** by the end of sixth grade. Carol's memory for visual detail was amazing, and she seemed to be able to appropriate the language of nineteenth-century novels into her own daily speech. Until I got around to reading **Vanity Fair** I had no idea that Carol was dazzling me with jokes and phrases she had cadged from Becky Sharp. Always, there was a brilliance to Carol's gift for mimicry. She ran rings around me that year and tortured me with the voices of Fagin and the Artful Dodger in the year Mom brought **Oliver Twist** home. The world of books was set for me by the intellectual hunger of my mother and the pure, exhilarating genius of Carol's use of the language. She could handle words I had never heard of with such naturalness that it seemed as if you were present at the creation of a language minted for your own pleasure. If I said that a sky was a pretty shade of blue, she would correct me, saying that it was lapis lazuli and only a simpleton would call it blue. She was ten when she pointed this out.

Among librarians, I was popular in every town I landed in until I got to Beaufort, South Carolina. It was another hellish year in my relationship with my father; his slaps would often bring me to my knees or knock me to the floor. My eyes were now dead giveaways, and nothing I could do could camouflage my visceral hatred of him. When I enrolled at Beaufort High School, it was my first sojourn into the world of public schools and neither of my parents liked the situation a single bit. Both acted as though my year among the infidels would cause a spiritual cataclysm that no sacrament or catechism could cure. My great problem was an incurable loneliness that had come to seem like a given. I didn't know a single soul when I walked into Beaufort High School, and I had no clear idea of what to do during the lunch break and recess in the middle of the day. At Catholic school, I could always wander into the church and pray. Beaufort High School convinced me that no church would provide me refuge during that particular year. On the breezeway separating the two wings of the school, there was an ominous gathering of the toughs and ruffians and popular kids. It looked dangerous as I passed through a ring of hostility and the mean laughter of teenagers who could send any strange new kid running for the hills. On that first day, not one kid said hello to me. By chance, I stumbled onto the library and I felt the deep pull of a homecoming as I walked into its silences. It was empty, abandoned. I now had a place to hide during lunchtime.

I looked around for a librarian but found myself in wondrous isolation. Moving toward the back of the room, I found a seat. Among newspapers and periodicals I took out the **Washington Post** and found out that Gonzaga High School had won its first football game that season. I'd have been a member of that team had my father remained stationed at the Pentagon. I wandered through the fiction section and pulled out Victor Hugo's novel **Les Misérables**. It was listed in the hundred books my English teacher at Gonzaga, Joseph Monte, had suggested we read before we went off to college. My mother, sister, and I were hard at work checking off titles from that sublime list. I entered the world of Jean Valjean and did not look up until the bell rang and the halls swarmed with students again. For two weeks I read **Les Misérables** without being noticed or discovered. Then Eileen Hunter stormed into my life.

In the halls of Beaufort High School, I'd heard rumors of Miss Hunter. She was famous among both teachers and students for her legendary temper and her need for absolute control of her book-lined fiefdom. Among students, the mere mention of her name inspired a sense of terror. She was known to be allergic to Juicy Fruit chewing gum, which inspired a certain breed of mischievous boy to plant wads of gum under tables and chairs throughout the library. If the chewed gum was fresh enough, Miss Hunter could be watched sprinting toward the teachers' lounge, where she would vomit in the sink. Trained as a teacher of home economics, she found herself recruited to be a librarian when there was a surprise resignation in the middle of the school year. When I encountered her wrathful gaze, she had served as the librarian for more than twenty years. Her disposition was troll-like and her demeanor combative. She seemed agitated every time a student disturbed the airspace of her private domain. When she spotted me reading Hugo she reacted as though I'd taken a box of Crayolas to the Book of Kells.

"What on earth are you doing here?" she said.

"I'm reading a book, ma'am," I said. In my high school years I was polite to the point of being oleaginous.

"I can see that. Do I look like an idiot or something?" Miss Hunter snapped. "It's against the rules for a student to use the library during lunchtime."

"Sorry, ma'am. I didn't know that," I replied.

"What's that book you're reading?" She grabbed it out of my hand and examined it as though it were pornographic contraband. She studied the book, then eyed me with a ferocious scowl.

"This book's never even been checked out. Are you reading it for the dirty parts?" she asked, as though she had cracked the mystery of this strange encounter.

"I didn't know it had dirty parts," I answered.

"If it does I'll toss it with the morning trash. If you find anything dirty report it directly to me. Hugo's a Frenchman. I don't like his books. You know what I hear about this Hugo guy?"

"No, ma'am."

"His characters," she said, studying the cover of the book. "He's depressing. All the folks he writes about are just so . . . just so miserable. We've got another one of his books. You ought to try that. It's about a football team. Do you like football?"

"Yes, ma'am."

Eileen Hunter seemed pleased at my answer and pulled another volume of Victor Hugo from a shelf. Then she handed me a copy of **The Hunchback of Notre Dame** for my reading pleasure. Though she never demonstrated a shred of affection for me, I heard from other teachers that Miss Hunter thought highly of me and always admired my passion for French literature.

Checking a book out of the Beaufort High School library required a swashbuckling, adventurous spirit, as Miss Hunter patrolled those aisles with the austerity of a knight-errant. Whenever she checked out a book, she treated the poor student as she would a visiting pirate. For Miss Hunter I think that the state of nirvana would be a library cleaned of all readers and the books all shelved and accounted for. As a librarian, she was legendary in all the wrong ways and for all the wrong reasons.

When I returned to teach at Beaufort High after my graduation from The Citadel, I encountered Miss Hunter again, but this time as a teaching colleague. She was as cranky and adversarial as ever, and would light into me with her complaints as I would bring four or five novels to check out for my weekly reading.

"I don't think teachers should be allowed to check books out of the library," she said.

"Pray tell why, Miss Hunter?"

"You're just taking a book out of circulation that a student might be reading," she harrumphed. She was a world-class harrumpher.

"They're all virgins. I checked. None have ever been checked out before," I told her.

"How dare you bring up the subject of sex in my library!"

"I only do it to excite you, Miss Hunter. Everyone has noticed your incredible sexual attraction to me. It's the talk of the faculty lounge."

"You repulse me in every fiber of my being."

"So you say, Eileen," I said, leaning toward her. "But I've read the secrets of your dark, disgusting heart. I know what you're really after."

"I'm calling Sheriff Wallace!" she said, "He'll shackle you like a dog and drag you behind his patrol car."

"Till our next forbidden encounter, Eileen."

"I didn't give you permission to call me by my Christian name."

"Eileen, Eileen, Eileen," I said as I sailed out to my first-period class.

My attraction to story is a ceaseless current that runs through the center of me. My inextinguishable ardor for reading seems connected to my hunger for story lines that show up in both books and the great tumbling chaos of life. Though I have not thought of the forbidding figure of Eileen Hunter for years, she recently roared back to me with her bizarre peculiarity intact. My genuine fondness for Eileen trumps my irritation at the thorny relationship she brought to the librarian's craft. I can forgive almost any crime if a great story is left in its wake.

Shortly after I began teaching in Beaufort I tried to read **The Complete Works of Charles Dickens**. Then I received a handwritten note from Miss Hunter asking if I could meet her in the library after school.

When I took a seat in front of her desk, I noticed that her pocketbook was open and that she was writing checks to pay her monthly bills. Though she did not greet me, she began talking as soon as I took my seat. "Conroy, I grew up in the country among country people. The finest people in the world. My mother and father were hardworking people and they raised me in the most genteel manner. They raised me to be a Southern lady with impeccable manners. Every inch of me is a Southern lady."

"What can I do for you, Miss Hunter?"

"I don't know if you've noticed it lately, Conroy, but I've come down with a summer cold."

"Should I drive you to a doctor? Or buy you some medicine?"

"That's the problem. Cold medicine never seems to work. At best, it has a placebo effect on me. My father was a gentleman farmer and he had theories about the common cold. He was famous in our neck of the woods for making his own remedies. Oh, this light bill is preposterous! He made a hot toddy which he claimed could cure even pneumonia."

"I don't see how I can help you."

"Be patient. Young men are so tiring when they let their impatience show. Now, a hot toddy would include many herbs and spices. But what makes them really effective is the addition of a shot glass of bourbon. In Beaufort it would be unseemly for a woman of my social standing to be seen entering a liquor store and emerging with a telltale brown paper bag."

"So you want me to buy you a bottle of bourbon?"

"A half gallon of Jack Daniel's Black. There

is a delivery box for Coburn Dairy beside my front door. Come after nightfall. Be discreet. There'll be an envelope with the exact amount of the purchase waiting for you. This is for medicinal purposes only. I've had trouble shaking this cold."

"How long has it bothered you, Miss Hunter?"

"I've had this cold for—let me try to guess—I couldn't produce an exact date, but I've had this summer cold for about the last twenty years."

It was the first and only joke Eileen Hunter ever shared with me, but I supplied her with cold medicine for the next two years, always with discretion and under the cover of darkness. Her loneliness seemed unbearable. In the years I knew her I never saw her reading a book or talking about a book she'd read. Her familiarity with literature was suspect, and she famously placed the Sherlock Holmes collection in the biography section. I can't approach the word "librarian" without her austere image rising in my consciousness. Even though she had a genius for being contrarian and disagreeable, there was an integrity she displayed in her fanatical need to control her small corner of the world.

Our relationship ended badly and it grieves

me to say it. She wore her Southernness like an impenetrable armor, and the integration of the schools was a constant agony to her. She could not hide her contempt for the black students and the personal injury she felt with the collapse of the Jim Crow laws of the South. Her relationship with the black students was venomous and her discomfort with them undisguised. She and I would clash often over her treatment of my black students.

"I'd like you to be fair to them, Miss Hunter," I said during one encounter.

"They've no right to be in my school," she said. "They'll get no special treatment from me."

"I only ask you to treat them as badly as you do the white students. That's not too much to ask."

"It's well known that you prefer the coloreds to your white students," she said. "It's the talk of the teachers' lounge."

"I like both; there's no harm in that."

"I've never liked the colored, Conroy. They scare me. Always have."

"Then try to get to know some of them. Try Grady Lights or Julia Buckner. They're the nicest kids you've ever met."

"You don't understand one thing about

the South Carolina way of life. You don't know what you're playing with. This colored thing's going to reach up and bite you."

And bite it did. In less than two years, I would be back in Miss Hunter's library addressing the Teachers' Association, trying to explain why I'd been fired from my job teaching black kids on Daufuskie Island. It was not my best day as a speaker, and my fury leaked in at the edges as I described my volatile year teaching those wonderful kids who didn't seem to have a chance to succeed in the world they were born into. Though I did not know it as I spoke in the library that was such familiar ground to me, I would never be hired to teach another day in my life. The teachers voted with a show of hands and they chose to support me by a wide margin. Eighteen teachers voted against me, all of them white, and all of them teachers I had known at Beaufort High School, all as colleagues and some who had taught me in high school. It nearly killed me to see Eileen Hunter's hand raised in support of my firing.

When it was all over, I had lost a court case to win my job back, I was in the middle of that white heat of creation that would produce **The Water Is Wide,** and I went to visit Miss Hunter at her home. I came in bright daylight so as not to alarm her. She cracked the door open and stared at me from the shadows.

"What do you want, Conroy?"

"There are no hard feelings, Miss Hunter. None at all. I came to tell you I understand why you voted against me," I said.

"I'd do it again."

"I know you would. But it's okay."

"I think you're a dangerous man," she said.

"No, you don't. I think you've always liked me."

"Then you've got another think coming."

"You know what's in my heart."

"I don't like what's in your heart."

"Yeah, you do," I said. "You still got that summer cold?"

I could hear her hesitate; then she said, "It comes and goes."

"Look in your Coburn Dairy milk case. I left you a bottle of Jack Daniel's. For medicinal purposes only, of course."

"Don't come back here, Conroy."

"It's okay, Miss Hunter. It's all okay," I said as I left. We never spoke again.

I was living in Atlanta when I heard Eileen Hunter died. I sent flowers to her funeral at the Beaufort First Baptist Church and had a Mass said for the repose of her soul. She had found me in her library, reading Victor

Hugo in 1961. I was born to be in a library and there wasn't a thing she could do to intimidate me or run me out. I think I was as fond of Eileen Hunter as anyone she ever met, and I believe she knew that. Despite her denials, I'll always believe she knew what was in my heart.

CHAPTER SIX

THE OLD NEW YORK
BOOK SHOP

I moved my family from Beaufort to Atlanta in the winter of 1973. Without quite knowing it I had become a controversial figure in Beaufort, an undistinguished fact that was disclosed to me at a neighbor's oyster roast in a backyard on the Point, the historic district. I had gone to high school with his children, and this lanky, outspoken man told me he had just finished reading my "nigger book." He'd tack my worthless hide on a barn door if I ever put him in one of my "nigger books," he said. When finishing up **The Great Santini,** I took immense satisfaction in the secret knowledge that I used this man's name for one of my characters, and that he would limp forever through my fictional world as a black man. But the encounter disturbed me and I was hearing rumors of my brothers and sister being hassled by sullen white students at the high school. By then, I was also certain that I had no chance to land any kind of job in Beaufort. I looked toward Atlanta as the place of my birth and the city that would allow me both anonymity and some measure of redemption.

In Atlanta, my wife, Barbara, and I bought a two-story brick house on Briarcliff Road near Emory University. Rather than work from home, I rented an office in a warren of haphazard rooms on the third floor of a Victorian house on Fifteenth Street. There was a lovely woman named Judy who had a seamstress shop in a guardhouse that protected the entrance to the house known locally as "the Castle." On the bottom floor was a small, intimate theater with smells of mildew and abandonment coming from the folds of its curtains, a place that delighted my imagination. I dreamed of writing a play that would open in that castoff theater, bringing the whole building back to some radiant, creative life. As I made my way to my office each day, I passed through a small village of marionettes, in all the suggestible muteness of their half-opened lifeless jaws. Here, I would continue the work of creating a fighter pilot and his long-suffering family. Though I'd begun the novel in Beaufort, I wrote the pilot's arrival from Europe at the Atlanta Naval Air Station, where I was born. I had the fictional family of the Meechams depart in the middle of the night from my grandmother's house on Rosedale Road. I imagined the trip to

Beaufort down those two-lane highways before interstates as they cut through pine forests and over rivers with Indian names. When
I finished writing for the day, I would make
my way down the unlit hallways watched by
the unhappy puppets who were my constant
circle of friends.

Since I am a man of ingrained habit, my
life has fixed points of immovable behavior
that can make my daily schedule seem neu-
rotic to the point of inertia. To me, the writing life requires the tireless discipline of the
ironclad routine. The writing of books does
not permit much familiarity with chaos.
Each morning I would leave my house just
after rush hour and make the ten-minute
drive to the Castle. I made the same journey
for months without detecting a nondescript
store on Piedmont Road that awaited my
notice and inspection. It was called the Old
New York Book Shop, and I drifted into its
unprepossessing interior in early April and
found myself released among a wonderland
of books that would utterly change my life. I
had first noticed the store for the most fatu-
ous reasons—in the mornings I passed a mis-
made, two-tiered trolley of hardbound books
for sale at a dime each. On the way back home
in the afternoon, the trolley would advertise
another sad grouping of books, each priced at

a quarter. The prices seemed insulting to any self-respecting book, hardback or not. Out of curiosity, I decided to check the store out, not knowing I was answering an invitation to my own interior fate in Atlanta.

At that time in my life, hardbound books were still an unaffordable luxury. I had never set foot in an antiquarian bookstore. By then, I had written two of the hardbound books on the modest bookshelves of my house. As earthly treasures, I had kept possession of my college textbooks and considered them highly prized mementos of my early years. My histories of England, my Norton Anthologies, and my works of Milton and Shakespeare satisfied some itch of acquisition in me. My favorite was **The World in Literature,** which I read after my graduation from The Citadel. That book introduced the works of Euripides and Catullus and Montaigne, those bright, singing names of writers whose works I'd never encountered and names I still couldn't pronounce. Though I had not excelled in my academic life in college, I had performed well in my English and history courses, yet still carried the unshakable thought that I was ignorant and unschooled. My mother's incurable sense of inferiority about her education would contaminate my own bloodstream and would cloud the arteries of self-esteem

in me for all the days of my life. I could read
a million books and still consider myself a
half-baked, mediocre thinker. But, by accident, I had discovered the nerve center of
my deliverance in a nondescript bookstore
in Atlanta. I had stumbled upon the secret
watchman of the most profound and illustri-
ous intellectual life I would ever experience.
Thousands of books roared out my name in
joyous welcome when I entered that shop for
the first time. Their presence both attracted
and intimidated me. Already my calling as a
writer had altered the course of my life, yet
the two books I'd written seemed anemic to
me, boilerplate at best, and I lacked the understanding, the sheer depth of culture I'd
need if I were to touch the sourceless, incan-
descent seas that roared inside me. I could feel
them but not set them loose; I could imagine but not articulate. As **The Great Santini**
began to form the storm warnings inside me,
my parents were covering the opening movements of their own tempest-tossed divorce,
and I found myself the reluctant chronicler of
their flawed, remorseless love for each other,
as well as the raw hatred that fed it. Whenever I wrote the word "Santini" it felt like a
razor cutting across a vein in my wrist. At an
early age, I had turned to reading as a way
for the world to explain itself to me. Here, at

last, I had stumbled into the store that would open up a hundred universities for my inspection. I had dropped out of nowhere and found myself at the gates of my own personal Magdalen College in Oxford. Here I could punt down the Cam through the hallowed grounds of Cambridge University, take notes on Balzac at the Sorbonne, rush to my morning class on Dante in Bologna, or sprint toward an honors class in Harvard Yard. The great writers of the world sang out in darkness and greeted me with the pleasure of my arrival.

Books are living things and their task lies in their vows of silence. You touch them as they quiver with a divine pleasure. You read them and they fall asleep to happy dreams for the next ten years. If you do them the favor of understanding them, of taking in their portions of grief and wisdom, then they settle down in contented residence in your heart. From Jane Austen to Émile Zola, all the great writers watched as I passed in careful review, walking the aisles of the bookshop. I paused at the four-volume set of Marcel Proust's **Remembrance of Things Past**. I had never heard of Proust or his magnificent literary achievement. Reading the first two pages of **Swann's Way**, I found the Moncrieff translation of the French magisterial but intimidating. The price for the complete set was twenty dollars, which at the time I thought was sinfully overpriced.

I entered into a maze of handmade, unpainted bookshelves; and I wandered through sections of poetry, British literature, general fiction, travel, nature, psychology, and American literature. It was during my slow voyage through this dusty labyrinth of a store that I experienced a lust for ownership that had never burdened me before. Though I'd always turned to books for completion and solace, I had become aware ever so gradually that I was one of those rare readers—I could change the direction of my life if the right book came my way to offer its subliminal powers for my inspection. The Old New York Book Shop would become the source of abundance where I would begin a lifetime safari on a headlong search for the great books of the world. If I were patient and observant, every celebrated book would pass by me on those shelves. That day, I bought three paperback books of literary criticism, but I was back the next day and the next. Familiarity with the store made me bolder; intimacy with the stock made me a collector. I began to buy in earnest, and the more I bought the more I wanted.

At the end of the first month I made my

first serious purchase at the Old New York Book Shop. I bought a lovely four-volume set of novels by George Sand, a French writer I'd only just discovered was a woman. The set was well made and exotic. The De Vinne Press certified that only two hundred fifty copies of this book had been printed on Dickinson handmade paper in August 1894. My copy number was one hundred thirty and the previous owner, J. H. Haven, had inscribed his signature on the first page of two of the four volumes. Later I would learn that his signature would render the book anathema to "real collectors," a defilement of the first order. To me, it added a personal touch because I got to admire the literary taste of Mr. Haven long after his death. The top edge of each volume was gilt and the fore edge untrimmed. It marked the moment when I became aware of the art of bookmaking. I found it a privilege to own such books, and I take immense pleasure at staring at them more than thirty-five years after I bought them in Atlanta.

Since I was certain that I'd like spending a lot of time in this store, my first order of business was to make friends with the owner. Cliff Graubart was a compact, muscular man who flitted about his store with the overwrought metabolism of a hummingbird. Though he was not unfriendly, he was withdrawn and unforthcoming and lacked the mannerliness that Southerners perform with such thoughtless grace. But my personality has always struck some people as too obsequious for their tastes. When I lived in Paris for a short time, some Parisians found my ebullience and sunny nature offensive to the very character of the city. In Minneapolis, I felt like a fireball as I tried to make friends with the Swedes and Danes who made up the inner circle of the poets and journal keepers in my sister's poetry circle. In the early days, Cliff treated me with all the suspicion of a trapdoor spider. From his early reaction to me, I could tell that Cliff considered the innate courtesies of Southerners a minor form of madness. He was also part of that innumerable tribe of outsiders who found Southerners stupid.

On my third visit, as I was paying him for a small stack of books, I said, "You never say hi to me when I come into your store."

"Hi," he said, unamused.

"What warmth, what charm!"

"You want a hand job instead?" he said as he wrote up the bill of sale. "I don't know you. I say hi to my friends."

"Would you like to know me?" I asked, extending my hand. He looked up at that hand as though I were offering him a live electric eel.

As we exchanged names, I asked, "Where you from?"

"You taking a census?" he said. "The city. New York City."

"I've heard of it."

"Good for you. Where are you from?"

"The city. Beaufort, South Carolina."

"That supposed to be a joke?"

"Yep."

"It ain't funny."

"But it's a start," I said.

And so it was. The friendship took off in the next couple of months and has continued to build momentum over the years. While I had assumed Cliff got into the antiquarian book trade to satisfy his own passion for reading, I could not have been more wrong. As I continued my own patient survey of his stock, I became gradually aware that Cliff was poorly read and that his starting up of a bookstore was more of a business opportunity than it was for literary enrichment. Though he could look up and reveal to me the value of any book, he had read remarkably few of them. He told me he had once had a first edition of **The Great Gatsby** that he had cataloged in his mystery section because it sounded like a mystery title to him. Plus, he'd never heard of F. Scott Fitzgerald. His self-education in the book business was "slow as humidity." It took him a good fifteen years before he felt as if he had mastered the trade. In the first month of our acquaintance, Cliff told me I'd never be a collector of books because I was too fascinated by reading them. A collector wants possessions, and a book in pristine, flawless condition that is displayed, but never sullied or contaminated by the barbaric act of reading itself. He told me that I had never noticed or remarked upon the condition of any book I purchased and hadn't bought a single volume that any self-respecting collector would allow in his library.

Since I showed genuine curiosity about what made a book collectible, Cliff had a stack of five books waiting when I next visited the store. He picked up a first edition of Robert Ruark's **The Old Man and the Boy**. He pointed to some light mottling at the edges of the boards and some light foxing to the endpaper. Shaking his head, he called the dust wrapper slightly rubbed and soiled. Next, he took the glassine wrapper off Wallace Stegner's **The Big Rock Candy Mountain** and showed me some light chipping to the spinal extremities and two short vertical tears at the crown. He showed me a first edition of Eudora Welty's **The Robber**

Bridegroom that was missing the dust jacket and had a half-moon imprint of a coffee cup on the title page.

Cliff said, "The only thing bad that did not happen to it was being tossed in the toilet."

In April 1973, Barbara and I threw our first party in Atlanta, gathering together both neighbors in the Emory area and writers I'd encountered at a dinner for Georgia writers that Jimmy and Rosalynn Carter held at the Governor's Mansion. That event felt like our arrival at the big time for Barbara and me, even though I still hear writers griping about the absence of wine or liquor. Several writers claimed they experienced delirium tremens twice during the course of the evening and that the lack of booze had disoriented them so completely that they'd been forced to eat the food. It was the night I met the writers Paul Darcy Boles, Paul Hemphill, Terry Kay, Larry Woods. I can still remember seeing the dazzling Anne Rivers Siddons coming down the corridor with her dapper husband at her side. For many years Annie had been an all-star writer for **Atlanta** magazine and its mercurial editor, Jim Townsend. The entire room turned around to watch her butterfly-like entrance as she joined the receiving line to shake hands with Rosalynn and Jimmy Carter. Annie was a Southern knock-out that night, and she would soon become one of the best friends I ever made. For more than forty years, we've supported each other and served as each other's head cheerleader, and she has represented a charming, centering force in my life. Many of the writers Barbara and I met that night with the Carters we invited to our first party on Briarcliff Road.

Cliff was the first guest to arrive. He surprised me by handing me a white pastry box wrapped in string. "I brought you some cake."

"Why?"

"Because that's the way you do it in New York."

Looking at the Atlanta skyline from my front porch, I asked, "Cliff, you noticed you ain't in New York anymore?"

"You got something against cake? Got something against eating? Hey, I was raised right. I wasn't raised in a potato-chip bag."

"What's in the bottle?" I asked him.

"Liquor. I hear that the goyim like to drink. So I brought you some liquor. It's a bottle of sake."

I took the bottle of sake and held it up to the light for inspection. "Hey, Cliff, you ever noticed I'm not Japanese?"

"Liquor is liquor." He shrugged. "The goyim are goyim."

Many of the people who attended that

distant and barely remembered party would become some of the great friends of my life. The party also marked a turning point in Cliff's life in Atlanta. I watched him move around the room meeting people and continually saying things that made these groups holler with laughter. He'd had a life of solitude since opening the bookstore and it took me several years to fathom the depths of his loneliness. Even though he had a natural instinct for comedy, he did not trust this gift to travel well when he migrated so far south of the Mason-Dixon Line. He had a natural distrust of the Southerner's willingness to incorporate a Brooklyn Jew's mannerisms into Atlanta social life. But Cliff possessed an unshakable, adamantine sense of friendship and he's something of a workaholic in the care and feeding and attention that he expends to keep his friends in an invisible circle around him. I learned that night that his father still worked in the fur district in Manhattan and was known as "the fitch king." His brother was born in Palestine, and his aunt Fanny had failed to escape Warsaw in time, so that she and her entire family perished at Auschwitz. That evening, Cliff would begin the career that would make him famous in the writing world around the South. Laughter followed him around the house that night as though he were spreading fairy dust over a lighthearted, pixilated world. When I visited the bookstore later that week, Cliff interrogated me as soon as I walked through the door. The party had enlivened him to the point of fascination.

"Hey, you told me you were a writer," he said, "but you could've bowled me over with a pubic hair when I found out you really were one."

"Why would I lie about that?" I asked.

"Don't know. I thought it was probably a pickup line. Something you might use to get laid."

"Southern girls like an MD after their husband's name. Or an 'esquire' on a bank account with lots and lots of cash in reserve. Writing books doesn't pay many bills."

"Barbara gave me this paperback as I was leaving," Cliff said as he handed me the Dell paperback edition of **The Water Is Wide** with an illustration of Jon Voight on the cover. "They've already made a film out of this one."

"Yeah. Don't know how that happened."

"Who cares? It means you're something. Not nothing like I thought when you walked in here with your dick in your hand. Something, not nothing. You get it?"

"You're treating me a thousand times better than you ever have, so, yeah, I get it."

"That crowd the other night. High rollers. Big shots. Movers and shakers. Wheelers and dealers. How'd you meet those highfalutin hoi polloi?"

"I told them you were going to be there," I replied.

Cliff bought a house at 1069 Juniper Street the next year, where he relocated the Old New York Book Shop, and I was part of the move. I remember arranging the poetry section in alphabetical order. This would become my second home in Atlanta for the next twenty-five years, and a time soon came when I realized that I knew where to find every book in the store. I was almost as familiar with the stock as Cliff himself was. My relationship with the books themselves began to change. Once, I shadowed only the literary sections in the front of the store, but I started to spread my wings. I found **Arabia Deserta** by Charles Doughty in the travel section, a coffee-table book with bright illustrations of the works at the Prado in the art section, and a facsimile edition of Audubon's birds in the nature section, all of which I added to my growing collection. I was on my way to buying between four and five thousand books from the Old New York Book Shop. I carried that bookstore with me wherever I went. I bought the books I had to have, and

I still regret the loss of the books I was thinking about when they were bought out from
under me by strangers who purchased some
precious items because of my hesitation or
unwillingness to write a check. I lost the collected works of Friedrich Nietzsche because
I needed to think about making such a large
commitment to the German philosopher. In
the same way I lost a set of Dostoyevsky and
a signed first edition of Nabokov's **Lolita**.
It took years of losing great books before I
quickened both my reaction time and draw.

Over time, I became acquainted with the
odd assortment of human fauna that com-
pose the most often glimpsed inhabitants
of a used-book store. It is a withdrawn sub-
species of marsupials, nocturnal by both in-
clination and habit, who drift through the
high branches of the book world. They tend
to be harmless creatures not automatically
drawn to chatterboxes like me. Out of habit,
I would begin conversations with them that
they would cut off in midsentence, also out
of habit. The "coffee man" would come in
once or twice a day to avail himself of the
free coffee Cliff handed out to his customers. Though the coffee man was addled and
unwashed and homeless, he struck a curious figure with me. He had a long key chain
that he decorated with discarded bottle

openers and house keys he would find as he searched through the trash cans of the city on his morning run. Not once in the twenty years we knew him did he utter a word to Cliff or me, but his solitude intrigued both of us and we could never agree whether we were invisible to the coffee man or he was simply buried alive in his own private world. His key chain would jingle when he walked, so I always heard him coming to look for me. Without saying a word or putting out his hand, he would wait for me to put some money on a bookcase near me. I would lay a one or a five or a ten before him. He would take the money, and I could hear him walk down the main hallway to the front door. If Cliff would allow it, he would sometimes consume a whole pot of coffee while standing guard at the coffee machine. He never looked at a single book, nor uttered a single word. When he stopped appearing, Cliff and I assumed he was dead. He was never heard from again. On occasion, when drinking a cup of coffee together, Cliff and I will toast the coffee man.

The bookstore could always provide a carousel of camouflaged tenants who would hide their bizarreness or social discomforts behind the shields of discarded books. For many of them, books were the lifelines to unbearable lives. They used Cliff's store as a travel agency that specialized in both disguise and escape.

In my drifting among the stacks of the Old New York Book Shop I would meet hundreds of people in search of that single book that would provide certainty as they looked to move ahead in troubled, dreamless lives. I met a pale, ethereal man who had exquisite taste in both literature and rare books, and he would entertain me with his shy but accomplished monologues on the works of Milton or T. S. Eliot. His intelligence was scholarly and precise, yet noticeably passionate when speaking of an unknown work of some obscure Romantic poet. He had developed an unswerving devotion to Algernon Swinburne and could recite sections of his poetry that made the language glitter in its stream of polished and opaline words. Cliff dimmed my affection for the starry-eyed man when he told me that my poetry-reciting friend, David, was one of the biggest shoplifters in Atlanta. Periodically, Cliff would banish him from the shop but David would come back, settle his accounts, and beg for reinstatement in a world that he couldn't live without. Later I would find rare illuminated books from old London publishing houses in the pet or travel sections and bring them up for Cliff to put under lock and key again. If you were scrupulous and patient in the hunt, you could find treasures that David had squirreled away in corners all over the store. I discovered a rare copy of **The Canterbury Tales** beside a diet book for pregnant women.

When I took over the shop for Cliff one day when he had a doctor's appointment, David stole the rarest book in the shop even though I didn't take my eyes off him a single time. His skills were so effortless that I became a fan of his uncanny aptitude for theft. Later, when David quit coming to the shop, we heard that he went off to die of AIDS, ashamed of his gayness and what his family's reaction to it might be. He never went to a doctor for treatment but simply retired from the world to die among his lovely, well-selected, and stolen collection of books. His taste in literature was impeccable, and he told me he had never owned a single copy of one of my books and had no intention of ever buying one. When I knew our friendship was on solid footing, David told me, "I wouldn't even steal one of your books, Conroy."

It delighted him to make me laugh, and Cliff and I always wished he'd let us help him during the cruel solitude of his death.

Whenever Cliff left me to run the store, I could read a book deeply and with no concern for the passage of time. Over the years

I'd gotten to know the regulars well and could even tell them if a new shipment of books in their specialty had arrived. In one of the first times I was running the store, an unprepossessing man with timorous eyes entered. He was looking for Cliff, and I told him that Cliff was having a drink with a cousin who had missed a plane at the airport.

"Can I help you instead?" I asked.

"Do you have any books on the torture and execution of Jews?" he said, looking around to observe whether he'd been overheard. "I collect books on the torture and execution of Jews."

"What a delightful hobby," I said. "Beat it, sir. And don't come back unless you hear we get a shipment of shinbones from Treblinka."

When Cliff bawled me out for insulting a customer, I protested that I enjoyed throwing the creep out and would do it again if I had the chance. Cliff then explained to me the nature of obsession and the peculiar habits or areas of interest that could stimulate men and women to pay him real cash. Of course, the man was an anti-Semite in the worst way, but there was no law against human stupidity. His real specialty was his belief that Jewish merchants had intermarried with Indian women as they traveled by the back roads between Atlanta and Savannah in the early days of the colony. These liaisons between Jews and women of the Cherokee nations resulted in American Jews having noticeable Asiatic tendencies.

"Okay," I said, "so the village dimwit thinks Jews have Asiatic tendencies because they mated with Pocahontas. What's that got to do with torturing Jews?"

Cliff said, "Hey, he's branching out. He's showing some intellectual growth. He's going to think I hired Elie Wiesel to run my cash register."

At a later time, I was manning the desk while reading **Long Day's Journey into Night** by Eugene O'Neill, and growing impatient with the play because I wanted it to be better than it was. I selected all my books for the possibility of some flare of candles along the road toward illumination or enchantment. Often the bookstore frustrated me when my own vast pools of ignorance made me pass by books that contained the real hard stuff I needed to make me dive deeper into the drop-offs in my own imagination. Though I was reading O'Neill's most accomplished play, he wore me down in gloomy rain forests of dialogue that seemed both exhausting and fruitless. But the moment froze when the front door opened and three large,

muscle-bound men walked into the store like
an offensive line breaking out of a huddle.
The largest man signaled someone outside in
a limousine and a lithe, watchful young man
with a terrific hat and expensive sunglasses
entered the store. When he asked me a question, he appeared shy as a mollusk.

"Do you have any books on freaks?" he
asked.

"We specialize in freaks here," I answered.
"You ever met the owner?"

"Cliff, isn't it?" the man said, looking at
me sidelong. "I bought some books from him
last time I was in Atlanta."

"First room on the right after the bath-
room," I said, pointing. "I know he bought a
collection of circus books last week."

"Circus freaks?" the man asked.

"I haven't checked them out. He's got a
couple of books on the Elephant Man."

"I bet I own them," the young man said.
"I tried to buy the skeleton of the Elephant
Man last year in England. They refused to do
business with me. It upset me very much."

"Those uptight limey bastards," I said.
I then went back to reading O'Neill, thus
missing any further opportunity to meet Michael Jackson. When Cliff told me who had
just bought several hundred dollars' worth
of books from me, I remembered the man's

hauntedness, but also his innate sweetness. Michael Jackson was simply another celebrity who proved that fame could damage a human soul without even breaking a sweat.

The most surprising daily visitor to the bookshop was my father, Don Conroy. If my father ever read a book for pleasure, he didn't share that information with his oldest son. He never bought a single book from Cliff unless it was a volume of my sister Carol's poetry or one of my books that he wanted to present to a new acquaintance. Compared to my well-read mother, Dad seemed illiterate and uninterested in the world of books. He found infinite hilarity in the fact that Carol and I were trying to make our livings by writing poetry and fiction. Though I can now see that my father suffered from a grievous psychic wound when my mother announced she was divorcing him, he displayed an awesome lack of insight into the role he might have played in my mother's radical surgery to excise him from her life. For so long Dad had played the insufferable jerk and disgraceful father that he had to learn new steps after he retired on the parade ground of Parris Island. I had loathed everything about him since I was a baby and had no compelling reason to recover a lost father I never had in the first place. My lifelong anger at him could turn into an incendiary fury by simply watching him inhale good Atlanta air. Each day, I was writing deeper and deeper into the life of my family with **The Great Santini,** and the nature of my betrayal of my own wounded tribe was becoming clearer to me. My own marriage to Barbara fell apart as I entered the deviant country of breakdown that would come to feel like some eccentric home place in the coming years. I fell into the abyss of **The Great Santini** and lost myself.

When **The Great Santini** was published in 1976, my entire family flipped out and went into a full fruitcake mode that lasted for many years. Grandma Conroy called me, pronounced me worse than Judas Iscariot, told me she would never speak to me again, and proved as good as her word. My father disappeared for three days and Uncle Willie called to tell me that he had gone somewhere to commit suicide and I had only myself to blame when they recovered his broken body at the foot of some ravine in North Georgia.

It was at the Old New York Book Shop that my father made his reappearance after his nightmarish retreat into himself to encounter my remorseless view of him as a man. Since his arrival in Atlanta, Dad had visited the bookshop every day, dropping in to gossip with Cliff about the town's writers. Cliff knew about my family's anxiety about Dad's withdrawal, so he followed Don into the sitting room for a cup of coffee. For his regular customers, Cliff had provided real coffee mugs with their names inscribed boldly on them. From a hook, Dad retrieved his cup that was embossed with the single word "Santini."

My father was agitated as he spoke to Cliff. "You see what that son of a bitch wrote about me?"

"Yeah, Don, I did," Cliff said.

"Why does he hate my guts?" Dad said. "Why would he make up those lies about me? Did you see what he said about me on page two twenty-one? Who could write something like that about his own father?"

"You didn't finish the book, did you, Don?" Cliff asked. "You poor dope."

"Why'd I finish a book like that? It's the worst book I've ever read."

"Hey, Don—it's the only book you've ever read," Cliff said. "But you've got to read the whole thing—then you'll know what Pat's really up to."

"He hates my guts; that's what he's up to."

"Listen to me, Colonel Dope. Pat wrote you a love letter. That's what the whole book's really about. He had to write it to find out how much he loves you."

"I wish he'd just written a letter or some shit like that," Dad said. "Shut up about this love shit."

"Take it for what it is."

"Hey, my eyes are getting moist. Knock it off about the lovey-dovey stuff. I like my version better. The kid hates me."

"The book lends itself to different interpretations," Cliff admitted.

My father's sensibilities remained hurt and raw for several years after the publication of my book, but Cliff had provided Dad with a line of reassurance that provided him with both a plausible explanation and an avenue of escape. For the rest of his life, people would ask him about his feelings about the book and my father developed a frame of literary references that extended from Cain and Abel, through Hamlet and King Lear, straight past the steppes of Russia with Leo Tolstoy, then backtracking to end his declamation with the nature of family tragedy as expressed in the fall of the House of Atreus. Where Dad picked up these reference points, I've no cotton-picking idea, but I'm dead certain that he never read a single line of any author he ponied up as providing either testimony or evidence in his defense. Later, he admitted that my sister Carol had contributed the House of Atreus, and he loved saying it out loud because it made him sound so goddamn smart. The biblical citations that would extend from Abraham to Isaac to a child's ingratitude being sharper than a serpent's tooth were pieced together from the religious educations of Father Jim and Sister Marge, the priest and the nun among my father's siblings. But Dad found that he'd developed a small passion for the more arcane and ostentatious displays of literary allusions. When challenged by a regular at the bookstore once on what my novel had to do with Hamlet, my father puffed up with aggravated malice and told the poor bastard to go read **Hamlet** again and it wasn't written into his job description that he had to explain the most profound intricacies of the Prince of Denmark to some poor illiterate "schmuck" in Cliff's bookstore.

Two months after the book's publication, Dad pulled up to Cliff's store and honked his horn until we emerged into the sunlight. Bobby Joe Harvey, my brother-in-law in Beaufort, had mailed Dad a bright red license plate that said, THE GREAT SANTINI. Bobby Joe had fixed it onto the front of Dad's car and there it stayed for the rest of his life. It became a familiar sight to commuters moving up and down Peachtree Street during rush hour. When Cliff gave me a book party to celebrate the publication of **The Great Santini,** he interrupted me as I was signing copies of my book, then walked me back toward the couch in the coffee room. Dad was drinking a cup of coffee from the Santini cup and signing my books with goodwill and humor: **I hope you enjoy my son's latest work of fiction**. He would underline the word "fiction" five or six times. **That boy of mine sure has a vivid imagination. Ol' lovable, likable Col. Don Conroy, USMC (Ret.), the Great Santini.**

The Old New York Book Shop and Cliff Graubart became famous in Atlanta circles for the book parties given for Atlanta writers in celebration of their newly published books. The tradition began when Cliff and I met a **Newsweek** writer named Vern Smith at a restaurant called the Mansion on Ponce de Leon Avenue. Vern was coming out with a novel about the primitive street life that had grown up around the drug trade in the ghettos of Detroit. Vern's dialogue was pitch-perfect, and he got a review from the **New York Times Book Review** that his kids should have laminated on his tombstone. The idea of a book party pleased Vern a great deal and he proved suave, friendly, and knowledgeable as we scribbled down a makeshift invitation list from all over the city. Because of Vern's solid connections in the black community, that first party was fully integrated, and the conversation was animated and good-natured. Vern was charming and vivacious as he signed more than fifty copies of his novel on that historic night. The only criticism I heard about that party, or any of the parties Cliff gave over the years, was the ghastly cheapness of the champagne that Cliff served from the rare-book room. I could calm the protests and claim out loud that the champagne was not cheap; it was merely undrinkable.

The parties always carried the aura of a debutante's ball as a new book would glide into Atlanta society, joining the easy fellowship of the thirty thousand books that stood in reverent attendance on these opening nights. Anne Rivers Siddons published her first novel, **Heartbreak Hotel,** the following year, and Terry Kay blazed forth with **The Year the Lights Came On**. The years began to gallop by as Marshall Frady signed books and later Paul Darcy Boles, Ted Turner, Frank Smith, Terry McMillan, Pearl Cleage, Joe and Doug Cumming, Jim Townsend, and Bernie and Martha Schein—there were dozens, then scores, then a hundred or more. Stuart Woods got his start here. Charlie Smith traveled down from New York to sign his novel

Caanan, taking advantage of the fact that he was a Georgia boy. Carl Hiaasen arrived for two book parties incognito to christen several novels he had ghostwritten. Cliff and I were in the bookstore when Howell Raines came in to tell us he had accepted a job as a reporter for the **New York Times** in the same year that he had the first and only double book party for the simultaneous publication of his novel **Whiskey Man** and his seminal book on the civil rights movement, **My Soul Is Rested**. Also in Atlanta, Wendell Rawls took the work that won him a Pulitzer Prize in journalism and turned it into a sledgehammer of a book called **Cold Storage**. Robert Steed, a lawyer at King & Spalding, published two books of hilarious essays. I would meet Griffin Bell studying books in the history section and Charles Kirbo and Jack Watson and other members of the Carter administration arguing politics as Ellis Hughes snapped the black-and-white photographs that would hang from the bookstore walls for the next twenty years. At times, Cliff and I would riffle through those expressive photos and encounter a whole country of strangers whose faces we knew but whose names have suffered a time-swept erasure for which there is no real cure. A pretty girl's face would flare in the faded light of chemicals and the busyness of dark rooms, sting us with the memory of her freshness, then recede again outside our lives. There is some deep wisdom in anonymity, in a nonnegotiable refusal to announce yourself after the pure insult of finding yourself forgotten.

The parties became social events; the gatherings assumed overtones that were provocative, even erotic. Flirtations could begin in the travel section and divorce be discussed within reach of Rilke or Saint-John Perse. Love affairs began near French literature and awkward rebuffed advances beneath the framed maps of colonial Georgia. I remember four pregnancies announced to applause, and a hundred telephone numbers exchanged, and two couples claimed they had made love in the attic. No writer ever read from a new book at those parties, because Cliff and I agreed that a writer reading from his or her own work was as boring as watching a race between snails. Atlanta children were conceived and born because their parents first caught each other's eyes as they purchased the books of friends and neighbors in a charged atmosphere that was both safe and seductive. I met governors and United States senators and mayors of Atlanta and civil rights leaders as they ascended the shapely stairs that led to the front porch of the bookstore. With Chet Fuller I talked about gardening and with Rosemary Daniell about having sex on a lifeboat. With Jim Landon I talked about his mountain-climbing expedition into the Himalayas and with Susan Raines, her remarkable photographs. The conversations were bracing, and the voices always seemed engaged. The talk began with books again, to the way the language formed in tongues in Atlanta with a river sliding on its western edge, and a granite mountain on guard duty to the north, with forests of dogwoods, with a nervous skyline always urging upward and a fleet of airplanes flung like stars against the night as the years moved past us in their awesome patience and their far more awful speed. The parties stopped in the early nineties. Cliff married Cynthia Stevens and they started a family and the parties started averaging about one a week. Routine and exhaustion set in; then the city exploded with a growth that seemed without reason or surcease.

In the year that **Cosmopolitan** magazine revealed that the Old New York Book Shop was the best and safest place for single men and women to meet one another, Cliff folded those book parties like linens and placed them on the shelves of time. In 1995, he gave one last party for me when **Beach Music** was published and my life was falling apart again. I considered it a great honor and a splendid act of friendship. Cliff and I noticed on the last night that no one who attended those legendary book parties in the early years could ever consider themselves youthful again. But by God, we were young in Atlanta once and managed to get a couple of things right.

I should leave it here, but I can't stop myself. Sometimes, when I return to Atlanta, I drive past the bookstore that Cliff closed many years ago and rented out to Einstein's restaurant next door. The store is empty now, unfurnished and inconsolable. One day it will be torn down and a thirty-story skyscraper will take its place. It was once the home of thirty thousand books, a village of lost souls who once held citizenship in a princely city of ideas where the bright glimmer of the English language formed a great wall before the assembled forces of chaos. In this store, there was once a time you could ask yourself the most necessary questions, and with patience and a discriminating eye you could receive an answer from one of the greatest writers who ever lived. The Old New York Book Shop was the cathedral where I staked out my own house of worship and learning.

Over the years, I took home thousands of books to refresh, replete, and sustain me, and sometimes, if I were lucky and alert, to knock my damn socks off. Now I look into its front windows and the store is bookless, soulless, and empty. It is a husk, a discarded snakeskin, an empty conch shell as mute as the sea. Though I come as a visitor, it is like visiting a beloved uncle with Alzheimer's. I was lucky to find this store when I was a young man, and I think I stole the dream of fire from the pillar of God when I found the books I was born to read. But it is voiceless now, and sad beyond commentary.

Over there to the left of the fireplace was the poetry section that I sorted through and pillaged on my endless voyage in search of that lucky strike where the words would drop down on me glittering, distilled, and perfect. From the poets I required an exquisite refinement where no hair was out of place—no cowlicks, no tangles, no mess. Standing off in that corner, I found the severe, humorless Gerard Manley Hopkins, who wrote symphonic, infinitely complex poems that were hymns to the earth. In the same spot I fell in love with and tried to memorize Dylan Thomas's "Fern Hill," which I found to be the most elegant prayer ever written, a hymn of God coughed up into his soft Welsh hand.

I bought five hundred books of poetry from the Old New York Book Shop and stumbled around in complete surprise that poets wrote for the sheer, unapologetic joy they took in creation. I came as a thief to the poet's ball. I envied the way they could make language smoke and burn and give off a bright light of sanctuary. The great ones could fill what was empty in me. In the vast repository of language, the poets never shout at you when you pass them by. Theirs is a seductive, meditative art. They hand you a file to cut your way out from any prison of misrule.

On my writing desk, I always keep the poets close by, and I reach for them when those silver, mountain-born creeks go dry or when exhaustion rearranges the furniture of my fear-chambered heart. The poets force me back toward the writing life, where the trek takes you into the interior where the right word hides like an ivory-billed woodpecker in the branches of the highest pines.

But I'm speaking of all the yesterdays that will not come again. The Old New York Book Shop has fallen asleep forever, locked up and desolate and wordless.

I sit on the top step watching the traffic on Juniper Street heading downtown. The drivers and their passengers do not have a clue what this place once represented in the history of ideas of this city. I'm not sure any of them would care. But if I close my eyes, simply close my eyes, I can bring it all back to rowdy, vivacious life. Once, the writers of a great city gathered here to celebrate the publication of our books. The lights shone bright and the doors were wide open and the cars would park all over the area. None of us were good enough to bring the English-speaking world to its knees. But we had a few things to say and we said them well. I turn to say good-bye to the Old New York Book Shop. But no farewells are necessary. The books I wanted followed me home. My God, the wonders I found there! Those same marvels cling to me and they will adhere and prevail as long as I can write a word, as long as I can dream a world from the silos of language inside me. So I bid a loving farewell to this wordless house. It was here I came as a young man and learned some things I needed to know. On its shelves, I found the old masters waiting for my arrival. When I die, my religion tells me I'll go to heaven, and I hope someone got that story right. I'll make a request that I get to live in the Old New York Book Shop on the night of a book party. I'll sponsor that party and welcome the guests as they arrive. Then I'll have the Atlanta writers gather around and I'll introduce them to a blind poet who would sit atop Cliff's desk. Through the mists and starlessness of time I'll clap my hands and bring the house to silence. Damn, it was hard to get those Atlanta writers to shut their mouths. But this is my party and a slice of heaven I think I earned. Then the poet will open his mouth at the resurrected Old New York Book Shop and I'll command him to sing his immortal words about the scrimmage of the gods, the terrible siege, and all the unbearable sadness of the fall of Troy.

Yes, we got some things right.

CHAPTER SEVEN

THE BOOK REP

In 1972, when **The Water Is Wide** was published, the sales representative, Norman Berg, made a visit to my home in Beaufort to offer valuable advice about how I was to conduct myself as a young writer making my way into the labyrinths of a business I didn't understand.

Until I met Norman Berg, I had not yet developed a philosophy of writing, nor figured out the strategies I would need to be a writer of consequence for many years to come. Norman lacked any sense of frivolity or lightheartedness when the subject was either books or the writing life, and his dedication to the world of language was like a pure stream inside him. He was a hard man who dismissed fools without conscience or regret. His mouth was a thin line underscoring a disapproving face, and it lay closed beneath his brow and nose like a lesser blade in a Swiss army knife. A meticulous man, he carried a love of order to extremes sometimes. His books were chosen and arranged with care. When a book he revered went out of print, he would republish it under his own NSB imprint. His volumes were jacketless but sturdy, and Norman displayed an almost religious affection for the books he rescued from oblivion. Because of the Norman S. Berg publishing house, I read **The Education of Henry Adams, South Moon Under** by Marjorie Kinnan Rawlings, **The Letters of Maxwell E. Perkins,** John Muir's **My First Summer in the Sierra,** and Frederick Ayer's **Before the Colors Fade: Portrait of a Soldier,** about George Patton. Norman was a passionate reader and an unflinching loyalist to those books and writers who had struck him with their inner brilliance. His reputation preceded him, as had warnings from editors and other writers cautioning me about Norman's pugnaciousness, his opinionated closed-mindedness, his caustic nature, and a negativity he could spread at will like a black pollen that could harm the confidence of any young writer. I ignored the warnings and welcomed Norman into my life. Since he would be the man pushing my books to Southern booksellers, it seemed reasonable that I make legitimate diplomatic inquiries into bringing Mr. Berg into my camp. I found his seduction effortless.

Like most men of wintry, implacable reputations, Norman was a solitary figure wounded by his own self-inflicted capacity to cut himself off from all opportunities of friendship. He had made a fetish out of solitude and a virtue of his impatience with small talk and his unwillingness to tolerate the company of the unread simpletons he encountered on his journeys throughout the South. The world of books was a sacred grove to him.

Because his personality was so off-putting and his manner so sharp-cornered, it took me years to welcome him into my life as a mentor and companion. Though he worshiped writers, he could not keep from trying to break their tender spirits and mold them into artists worthy of his dark imprimatur. His championing came with a price. From the very beginning Norman longed to turn me into a writer I was never born to be. It was Norman's deepest wish that I take a thousand pages of my overcaffeinated prose and cut it down to a hundred pages of glittering, hard-boiled writing that would shine in its elegant completeness. He wanted me to write a book using all the delicacy and craft of watchmakers hunched over springs and wheels as tiny as semicolons. My attraction to the colossal and the elephantine offended him. Like many editors before and after him, Norman became a head cheerleader for restraint and economy of style. Ever since the English language in all its vertiginous, high-hurdling glory had been passed down to me by a word-stung mother, I had enjoyed getting my hands dirty anywhere the language would grant me a letter of transit. Norman would argue for the elegance of understatement. Countering, I made what I thought was a compelling case for overreaching, the wonders a writer could coax from his or her talents if they approached a blank page with their imagination afire and unbound.

"Don't you want to matter?" Norman Berg asked me on the veranda of my house on Hancock Street in Beaufort. "Don't you want to be part of the literary discussion? Don't you think about your place in literature?"

"No, I haven't thought about any of that, Mr. Berg."

"Then what do you want?" he asked me. "Why are you doing this?"

"Because I want to be remembered."

"You don't write well enough to be remembered."

It was not the last time Norman Berg would hurt my feelings, but I thought his early criticism would offer a firewall when I made my timorous way in the world of New York publishing. From the earliest days of our friendship, he brought me books that he believed I should read before daring to impose my own puny visions on an unsuspecting American public. Norman brought me the books of new writers who had impressed him with their debut novels. Because of Norman Berg, I had read Philip Roth's **Goodbye, Columbus,** Don DeLillo's **Americana,** and Paul Theroux's **Waldo** before I was published by their publisher. I felt then and I feel now a deep affinity with those writers who appeared in that first fall list with me. Each time he would visit me from Atlanta, Norman Berg would bring me dozens of books, and I could gauge his pleasure as he quizzed me about each author, making sure I could present ample evidence that I had read every book he brought into my house. When he quizzed me about the contents of a book, there was always a competitive sting to the queries. Books seemed to bruise rather than edify him. Because they were true to life, they could seem harmful to Norman, as though he were picking up live jellyfish from a tidal pool. There could be no mastery or understanding without pain. Whenever we sat down to discuss literature, I knew he would tolerate no introduction of frivolity into the conversation. Books were a matter of life and death in the world of Norman Berg. He was an easy man to dismiss and a hard one to love. In the end, his great solitude tamed me.

In the spring of 1972, Norman picked me up in Beaufort and took me on a sales trip through the Carolinas, and beyond. He wanted me to understand the world of bookselling from the top down, so he insisted that I accompany him on a trip where he would sell my book **The Water Is Wide** to stores around the South. He instructed me to study the fall list and to hunt for clues that would let an owner know how important the publisher considered my book to be in the grand scheme of the fall season. According to his reckoning, my book was the tenth-most-important book that would be published in the next sales cycle.

"Your book's not a big-ticket item for Houghton Mifflin," Norman said. "I can guarantee you that much. How many copies are in the first printing?"

"I don't know," I said.

"You make it your business to know. Your agent should've told you. The first printing's only five thousand copies. It won't even sell that many."

"How do you know?"

"Experience," he said. "You want to know about books. I deal in cold facts."

He drove me to Charleston, where he let

me sit in as he sold his fall list to the Book Basement and the two elegant men who ran the store in the shadows of the College of Charleston. Since I had gotten to know the men slightly as a cadet and had become a regular customer since my graduation, I was relieved when they ordered five copies of **The Water Is Wide** and irritated when Norman tried to talk them into reducing their order to three books.

"You can always reorder," Norman said.

"Mr. Conroy's firing was covered well in the press," the first man said. "We're comfortable with that order."

Next, we drove over to King Street and I entered Hugeley's bookstore, a much larger venue than the Book Basement. Hugeley's bristled with Citadel connections, so they had never ordered a single copy of **The Boo,** my self-published book that rankled the rare sensibilities of the Citadel power structure by my championing a commandant they had fired for his corrosive effect on discipline within the corps of cadets. Mr. Hugeley was detached rather than personable when he met me that day, but he ordered two copies of the book, which felt like a victory of the smallest sort to me.

"You made enemies at The Citadel," Norman said as we walked back to his car.

"It wasn't hard to do."

"Why would they get mad over **The Boo**? It's unreadable. A piece of shit is the best thing you could say for it."

"It's mine. That's the best I can say for it."

"No," he said. "It's yours and it's the worst thing you can say for it."

At night we camped in his Airstream trailer and he always tried to choose campgrounds where he could hear the sound of flowing water. He also loved the sound of an agitated surf or the struggle of an incoming tide as it surged against the wind—against the hardened shoulders of a Carolina sea island. He cooked quail and rice and gravy on a propane stove. At night, he talked about the books that had changed his life. He had ordered a case of wine, a Chianti, and he insisted that we drink from fine stemware and eat our meals on good china. Always, Norman pulled guard duty for the importance of civilization as a cure-all for the encroachments of chaos into the human condition. Before he cut out the lights, he would play recordings of Mozart's piano concertos as we read from books he collected in the small but well-considered library he had gathered for our sales trip into the American South. It was somewhere outside of Spartanburg that Norman discovered that I had never read the works of J. R. R. Tolkien and he launched into an aggrieved monologue about my lack of preparation to embark on my life as a writer without a working knowledge of Tolkien's great descent into the dense mythologies of his own imagination. Armed with a hard-earned ignorance that I tried to camouflage with bravado, I foolishly argued that Tolkien wrote books for children and a cult of frothy adults who never took the time to grow up. With considerable skill, Norman eviscerated every argument I threw at his windshield as I tried to break the stranglehold of a writer I'd never read. He trounced me soundly as he introduced me to the many pleasures of Middle-earth and the immeasurable courage of hobbits. As he dragged me through the perils of Frodo's quest, he spoke of the dark and brutal authority of the ring of power, and the gathering of the ceaseless evil in Mordor. I didn't know a single thing Norman was telling me about and my embarrassment over being caught in such a bald-faced, unnecessary lie stung me deeply. But I let Norman's passion for Tolkien steady me. In an endangered land of dwarves and elves and wizards, I listened to the story of creation and the unseen world told once more by a writer with supernatural, unsurpassable gifts. I let the story possess me, take me prisoner, feed me with the endless abundance of its honeycombed depths. It is a story that rules me. In our modern age, there are writers who have heaped scorn on the very idea of primacy of story. I'd rather warm my hands on a sunlit ice floe than try to coax fire from the books they carve from glaciers. Writers of the world, if you've got a story, I want to hear it. I promise it will follow me to my last breath. My soul will dance with pleasure, and it'll change the quality of all my waking hours. You will hearten me and brace me up for the hard days as they enter my life on the prowl. I reach for a story to save my own life. Always. It clears the way for me and makes me resistant to all the false promises signified by the ring of power. In every great story, I encounter a head-on collision with self and imagination.

Though Norman Berg was not a good storyteller, he carried the day with his ringing, high-strung defense of Tolkien's works. Outside the hills surrounding Asheville, Norman told me that a good novelist wrote about the whole, known world each time a word was written on a blank page.

"You claim to be writing your first novel." Norm said it in a voice that let me know he didn't believe me.

"I have," I said, having written the first

pages to the book that would become **The Great Santini**.

"Does it tell me everything I need to know about leading a good life?" he asked. "And I mean everything."

"No."

"Then throw it away. It's not worth writing."

"I'm twenty-six years old, Norman. I don't know everything in the world yet."

"That is good," he said, softening. "At least you know that much. Keep writing. If you're lucky you'll have one or two important things to say before you die."

"Here is one of them," I said. "Fuck you, Norman."

His laughter took us all the way to the campsite outside Asheville. I discovered early that he liked it when I fought back wherever his distemper turned surly or mean-spirited. He found my resistance to his manifesto on literature stimulating when he talked about books. Self-doubt was a country of origin to me, but Norman entertained no such uncertainties about himself. He believed that good writing contained the irrefutable answer to every question that could plague mankind's toilsome journey beneath the stars. Before we went to sleep at night, he would walk me out to show me a full moon, its silver captured in the tossed slipstream of a mountain river. "Always know which phase the moon is in," he would say. "Keep up with the transit of planets. Know everything. Feel everything. That's your job as a writer."

"What's your job, Norman?"

"To suffer. To feel everything in the world. But it dies inside me. I have no gift. I can't write. That's why I'm driving you crazy."

On that trip, Norman cut a deal with a bookseller somewhere in the mountains, maybe Virginia, maybe Tennessee. I was struck blind by the impetuous desires of my own ego in those days, and the wonderfulness of my own self. Norman walked me into a small store on a hilly street and introduced me to an elderly man who seemed less than dazzled at the prospect of meeting me. In fact he was brusque, discourteous, and I took an instant dislike to him. I could tell he wasn't about to write to his mother about his good fortune in meeting me. Then Norman Berg tossed a surprise in my lap that still amuses me almost forty years after it happened. At the time, I felt bushwhacked and sold down the river. Norman had just sat down in the back room of the bookstore to sell the fall list when he tossed his notes and paperwork and catalogs toward me.

"You've seen me do this, Pat," he said. "You sell the list. Let's see if you've got what it takes to be a book rep. We know you can write a book; now let's see if you can sell one."

Though I protested such a slick betrayal, I was caught up in the imaginativeness of the setup and the boldness of the jest. Mimicking all that I had seen Norman do for a week, I launched into a sales spiel for the most important books on the list, the books the publisher had the most invested in and whose success the future of the company depended on for its financial health and survival. I made the case for the nonfiction books by John Kenneth Galbraith and Arthur Schlesinger and wrote down my first two orders, which were modest though respectable. Turning to the novels on the list, I delivered thumbnail sketches of the pleasures each book provided, though I've a slender memory of not having read a single work of fiction that I was attempting to sell to the crusty man who cleared his throat in annoyance with every presentation I made. Finally, I came to the existential moment when I was offering my own book **The Water Is Wide** for this unpleasant man's impartial judgment. I described a young man going to teach on a Carolina sea island back in 1969, the first white teacher who ever taught black children in that part of the world. The kids were in terrible trouble, but the man thought he could teach them and make a difference in their lives.

Even I could decipher the amateur quality of my presentation, but I got surprised in the middle of my delivery when the man said, "Who gives a damn?"

"Excuse me?" I said.

"I don't care. What should my readers care what happened to a bunch of black kids on an island no one's ever heard of?"

"The book is kind of well written," I said.

"Kind of? It's kind of well written? That'll stir the souls of my readers. It sounds like a total bore. Pass."

"Pass?" I echoed.

"Yeah. Pass. I don't want to order a single copy of that book. It's not for me. I can't think of a soul who'd buy it."

"But there's a publicity campaign that's pretty good."

"Pretty good? Not good enough. I pass. Let's go on to the next book."

I finished selling the list in a barely controlled rage and gave a shameful performance in presenting the backlist, which I always found impressive. By the time I left that bookstore, I was ready to whack the living daylights out of that smug, hostile bookseller who had taken such grotesque pleasure in my humiliation.

"You set me up, Norman," I complained over dinner that night.

He laughed and said, "I sure did. I thought you were too smart to fall for that little trick. I was wrong."

"You knew he was going to pass on my book."

"Yep, I set it all up. He didn't own that store. He's a retired rep. Did it as a favor to me."

"What's the point?"

"You're the only writer in America I know of who's ever sold a list for his publishing company," Norman said. "It makes you rare. Time will tell if it makes you exceptional."

"I still don't get it."

"Now you know how hard it is. Reps are going into bookstores all over the country trying to sell your books. No one knows who you are. No one gives a shit. Your book depends on the reps falling in love with your book. They've got to fall in love with your language, your story—they're selling the spirit that lives in your book. If it has a spirit."

"Why didn't you get him to order at least one copy of my book?"

"Because then it wouldn't have hurt so

much," Norman Berg said. "Hurt is a great teacher. Maybe the greatest of all."

When Norman dropped me off at my house in Beaufort, he handed me a package roughly wrapped in butcher paper. I did not unwrap the gift until I sat at my writing desk the next morning. Inside, there was a boxed set of **The Lord of the Rings** by J. R. R. Tolkien. Norman had included a brief hand-written note that told me he treasured our time on the road together, that he thought I was on a quest to be a writer that mattered, and that I must read and remember every-thing. He believed that the writers of the world were ring bearers who bore the weight of the world on their shoulders, but I would understand his meaning only when the ring of power disturbed my art and rose up to trouble my quest. Norman then revealed to me that he didn't consider any writer edu-cated until they had absorbed the radiant wisdom of **The Lord of the Rings**. For the next month, I joined the fellowship of souls who followed the hobbit Frodo on his peril-ous journey into the dark lands of Mordor. I mark the time I spent reading those splendid books among the richest days of my life. The great books are like the elevation of the host to me, their presence transformed, their ef-fect indelible and everlasting. What is the loss of a job, the death of a friend, or a bad review when you've followed Gandalf the Grey through the mines of Moria and the march of the Tree-folk on Isengard?

When Norman Berg came to Beaufort for the celebration of the publication of **The Water Is Wide,** I walked him out onto the second-story veranda of the only house I'd ever written books in.

"Gandalf the Grey," I said, raising a glass to him. "I finished the trilogy."

"If you think I'm Gandalf the Grey, you got nothing out of the book."

"You bought me the book," I said. "You brought me news of the ring."

"What'll you do with it?"

"Ask me on my deathbed."

"I won't be here."

"I sure hope not."

"I don't think you'll ever be a writer," he said. "I don't think you've got what it takes."

"But I've made some great friends along the way," I said. "Guys like you."

He sniggered, but his laugh was as joyless as it was noiseless. His critical powers always overwhelmed his creative ones, and he writhed in his own awareness of this indisputable fact. As we rejoined the party downstairs, I watched as Norman erased himself as he entered into the company of my friends and well-wishers. Later, I would learn that he never introduced himself to my wife or mother or friends. Later, he claimed he loathed parties because it represented time stolen from his priestlike engagement with the great literature of the world. In public, my impenitent good cheer can strike even my closest friends as a bit on the sunny-side-up spectrum of human behavior. Norman considered my affability as an incurable flaw of character that would prove fatal to my pretense of becoming an artist. Without saying good-bye, Norman Berg left town early the next morning.

A year later, I moved my family to Atlanta, where I rented a series of offices in the midtown area that failed to fire the imagination as I began to take a withering look at my brutalized childhood. The betrayal of my father was not an effortless production, and I began a long, quiet nervous breakdown as I described the abysmal sound track of my boyhood. At this critical juncture, Norman Berg invited me out to his farm, which he called Sellanraa.

When I stepped out of the car that day, Norman and his wife, Julie, were working in their vegetable garden. A pack of bird dogs bellowed from their unseen cages in the rear of the great, weathered barn. The Bergs lived on fifteen well-tended acres bordered by a forest of oaks and pines that gave them the illusion of having escaped the land rush that had consumed the Atlanta suburbs. Inside the house was a great room with a flagstone floor, a massive rock fireplace, and a library of five thousand books near the door to Norman's warren of offices. On this day, Norman removed a book from its shelf. Whenever he presented me with a book, it had a ceremonious feel, as though he were laying a sword on my shoulder inducting me into an ancient brotherhood.

The book was **Growth of the Soil** by the Norwegian writer Knut Hamsun. The copy he gave me had once belonged to Norma M. Saylor, who lived in Palmyra, New Jersey.

"It's an essential book. A necessary one," Norman Berg said in his throaty catechist voice. "It's the most important book I've ever read. I named my farm Sellanraa in honor of Isak, the man who builds his home and raises a family out of nothing."

"I'll read it."

"You don't just read this book," Norman said. "You must enter in. Live it. It contains the great truth."

"Which is?"

"Everything of virtue springs from the soil. Civilization always comes along to ruin it.

But you can always find the truth if it comes from the earth."

"It sounds like the most boring book ever written."

"Read it. Then decide." He walked me out of the house and led me across a broad greensward that led to the original farmhouse—a simple, two-bedroom house with books and paintings and a working kitchen. It had a fireplace and a cord of wood for burning. There was a writing desk with pens and ink and the yellow legal pads I liked to write on stacked in a neat pile.

"Julie and I would like to offer this as an office to complete your novel. We won't get in your way."

"You have to let me pay you some money," I said, moved by the gesture.

"Complete your novel," he said, "and that will be payment enough."

I read the book **Growth of the Soil** before I began the final sprint of my own novel. An anonymous man appearing in the wilderness and building a life out of nothing except his own strength and ingenuity was a sacred myth of origin to Norman Berg. It described an unattainable life for him, a misplaced horizon that no longer existed without compromise. The book was dense with power and a sense of mystery that literature slings like pollen when some writers turn toward art. Knut Hamsun rose out of the dark forests of snow-haunted Norway the way J. R. R. Tolkien took his malice-haunted journeys in Middle-earth. Norman liked books that permitted no commerce with the age we were living in at the present time. At Sellanraa, his solitude began to make sense to me. He was engaged in a long, obstructionist quarrel with the world. He found most of modern life unbearable and the rest indefensible. It did not take me long to realize that Norman was trying to recruit me in some rearguard action during the long retreat from a sense of invisible order.

In the first month of my residency at Sellanraa, I gained control over the themes that would carry **The Great Santini** to its conclusion. Writing would always seem like a form of coal mining, with its descent into the black hearts of mountains and the long journey back to the light where fires could flourish in honor of your patient, hardscrabble labors. I wrote myself into a fever pitch as I approached mania, then meltdown.

As I came toward the end of the book, I stayed at the farmhouse for weeks at a time. Each night, Norman would walk down to ask me for dinner. Julie was reading Walker Percy's book **Lancelot,** and she spoke about

the book with affection and some delight.
Norman gave a reader's report on the books
he was reading for the upcoming sales conference, including a book by Paul Theroux and
one by a new writer, Henry Bromell. After
dinner Julie went to bed and Norman and I
sat in two enormous chairs next to his huge
stone fireplace in the vast sitting room. The
books stared down on us. We sipped glasses
of wine, and Norman asked me to read something from the novel. I read a section I'd been
working on that week about a Little League
coach of mine named Dave Murphy. After
showing me great kindness and patience during a memorable summer, Dave died the
following year of a terrible cancer. As I read
that night, I thought it was the best piece of
writing I had ever done. I read it and I read
it well. Wordless as usual, Norman stared at
the fire and it was several moments before he
spoke.

"You're never going to be a great writer.
Not even a good one. You can aspire to mediocrity. Nothing else," he said to the flames.

"You've been clear about that."

"But you're going to have moments. Like
that one. That was a moment," he said.

"You liked it?"

"I didn't say that. But I know a lightning

strike when I see it. I can only read. Never write."

"Ever tried?"

"Of course. But I was born blind and deaf. This is not Sellanraa I'm living in. It's a tomb and an iron lung."

"Oh, Mr. Uplift enters the room again."

"No, the truth teller. The man with nothing."

I came to the last chapter of **The Great Santini** and I wrote it in one marathon sitting that took a full twenty-four hours of rough labor. Because he knew I had come to the end, Norman would tap on the back door with great discretion, and I would find a hot meal and a book on the doorstep. He left me **The Pisan Cantos** by Ezra Pound, **Deliverance** by James Dickey, and **Two Years Before the Mast** by Richard Henry Dana. When I finished killing my fictional father, I staggered down to the main house at Sellanraa for a celebratory meal. He took me to the forest on his land and loaded a shotgun for me to hunt squirrels for dinner. The shotgun was beautifully made and had intricate carvings on its stock of scenes from **The Yearling** by Marjorie Kinnan Rawlings. By then, Norman had told me the sad, desultory tale of his distant love affair with Ms. Rawlings.

He admitted to being tyrannical and heartless about her writing, and that he nearly drove her crazy with his disapproval of her last novel, **The Sojourner**. He had become a nightmare in her life and he now believed she could've written several more books if she'd never met him. As he cleaned the squirrels I had shot, he confided in me that Marjorie had been the great love of his life.

After we ate that night, Norman took a picture of me sitting in a chair in the kitchen of Sellanraa. It became the author photograph on the back of the book jacket of **The Great Santini**. Norman refused to take credit for the photo, but I treasure it for what it has come to represent to me. When he died, I delivered his eulogy. I held a copy of **Growth of the Soil** as I delivered the final words to this loneliest of men who became dizzy with his devotion to literature and writers. Though he could not banish that juiceless critic whose judgments were cutting and ruthless, he never uttered again the word "pass" when my books came into the conversation. As I write this, I own the shotgun that Norman had made for Marjorie Kinnan Rawlings. I don't know where he is buried, but I hope it is somewhere in Georgia.

CHAPTER EIGHT

MY FIRST WRITERS' CONFERENCE

When I finished my first novel, **The Great Santini,** I experienced no cleansing sense of accomplishment or completion. For reasons that have always been unclear to me, the books inside me seem to reach some unanimous agreement about which one of them will go to the head of the line as I open up the next artery that surges out in a tidal fury from the headwaters of my interior. With **The Great Santini,** I had loosed some unspoken furies from the grottoes pooling beneath my family story. Though I had earned an unmerited reputation for loyalty, my family and many of my friends were about to encounter false effigies of themselves crafted from my sulky, hotheaded imagination. I was about to piss off nearly all of my closest relations and a goodly portion of the best friends I had ever made. I felt like I had put a gun to my family's head and pulled the trigger. I needed the companionship of other writers and the comfort of other books. A friend of mine who was a poet, Betsy Scott, called me at that perfect moment to say she had signed me up for a writers' conference that was taking place the following week at the Callanwolde Fine Arts Center, in Atlanta. Betsy and I had both loved the book **Diving into the Wreck,** and Betsy told me that we were going to a poetry workshop led by Adrienne Rich. Then Betsy thrilled me even further with a murderers'-row list of writers who would be at the conference, including William Gass, Alice Walker, David Madden, Miller Williams, and Maxine Kumin.

As I look back on that period of my life, I get no sense of myself as being a young and callow man or any sense, mordant or satirical, of time passing. The years can be seen as hourglass-shaped or demon-driven or diamond-backed, but I can recall no sense of alarm at the slipstream passage of time. I could discern time's easy spillage, its queenly dogwoods in the snowy plumage of late April, and the annual road races that always seemed to end near the azalea banks of Piedmont Park. Though I had published two books, I could not yet get myself fitted with the green jacket that would identify me evermore as a Georgia writer. Since I had not published a work of fiction, I could not yet call myself a writer. When I read the galleys of **The Great Santini** my claims for myself seemed fraudulent and overblown. I had never hung around with writers of national renown except for the single semester that I sat in the classrooms of James Dickey as he spoke of poetry as the most important thing on earth. From Dickey, I took to heart the lesson that ambition should always serve as the handmaiden to talent. If you possessed any talent at all, you should do anything to nurture and heighten it. He encouraged us to read the great books, to develop the most remorseless and unforgiving critical eyes, and to encounter the great writers and personalities of our time. Because of Dickey's own outsize personality, he often stalked about our classroom caught in some strange country where a word-crazed lumberjack could raise his own hybrid breeds of hothouse flowers. Though I revered his poetry and marveled at his novel **Deliverance,** James Dickey provided me with a lifelong distrust of other writers. The world of writers was a snake hole, a circle of hell—a rat's nest and a whirlpool and a dilemma—not just a world. Dickey was vindictive and combative enough to enjoy the border skirmishes that often broke out among the poets he admired the most, and those he held in unutterable contempt. His example proved fruitful to me. I've spent most of my life avoiding the companionship of writers.

I try never to be rude, just seldom available. Though I have met some of the great writers of our time, I've become good friends with very few of them. The tribe is contentious, the breed dangerous.

The estate of Callanwolde had played a bit part in my family saga. Its vast acreage abutted my grandmother's house on Atlanta's Rosedale Road, the home my mother brought me to after my birth. Callanwolde was a baronial Tudor mansion occupied by a branch of the Candler family, the mythical race who enriched themselves by putting their faith in the healing powers of a sugar-water called Coca-Cola. In Atlanta, they were a race of kings. My mother and grandmother spoke of them as though they composed the modern-day court of Medicis. During the year my father was away fighting in the Korean War, I attended kindergarten at Sacred Heart School by day and roamed the forests of Callanwolde when I got home. My pretty young mother drew the attention of a seven-foot pervert who would try to break into our house two or three times a week to get to her. Whenever the police were called, we would watch the seven-foot-tall man sprint into the forests of Callanwolde. I would eventually use the story of the giant, whom we called "Callanwolde," in **The**

Prince of Tides. The place held terrifying associations for me.

Betsy Scott was a lovely young woman from Spartanburg, South Carolina, whom I had met at Emory when she was studying poetry under Michael Mott. She and I entered the writers' conference together, and saw that my friend Cliff Graubart had saved seats for us near the middle aisle as Dr. John Stone conducted the opening ceremonies. Over one hundred fifty writers had signed up for the conference, billed as the largest convocation of writers ever assembled in Georgia. At that time, I think I was ready for some writer to utter the mysterious words that would open up the portion of my imagination where the great unsayable secrets lay in hiding. I was looking for a companionable guide who would steer me toward the right channels and show me the books that would both whet my ambitions and teach me to regulate the brush fires that could burst loose into whirling infernos of language. My search was clear. I was hunting for a teacher who already had the prestige of arrival and did not fear the role of mentor to a younger, less accomplished writer.

In the first session that afternoon, I was part of a short-story workshop taught by the intimidating William Gass, whose book

Omensetter's Luck I had read in anticipation of his class. He had great bravura and showmanship, but he carried an intellectual freight that seemed to interfere with both his writing and his teaching. He intimidated his class with the brutish authority of his intellect. Ideas seemed to excite him more than his own writing did, and certainly the writing samples the class had given him. He carried more poisonous quills in his vocabulary than a porcupine did on his back, and his assessments were often cruel, even if just. He was neither wishy-washy nor mealymouthed, and you could feel the grand deflation in the room as wounded egos began to die. In a final tally, I thought Gass had a grand intellect, but a shoddy heart. At the end of his session, he clashed with a young woman who had written a short story about her lesbian lover. She fought back with much gusto when Gass accused her of writing emotional, hysterical tripe instead of literature. Later, it pleased me immensely when her story won the first prize as best in the show. I found Gass to be dyspeptic and prickly, as though he had not figured out how to wear his fame. Or maybe he thought he had not earned quite enough of it.

When I walked down the long lawn to my car, I ran into Rosemary Daniell and a group of four other women writers. One of them I recognized as the Georgia novelist Alice Walker, based on her photo in the program. I was also carrying a copy of her latest novel, **Meridian,** which I had liked and wanted her to sign for me.

Rosemary and I kissed and said hello, looking like lovers who'd been separated for years. Rosemary is a wide-eyed voluptuary who is as sexy and flirtatious as any woman I've ever met. She is the kind of girl a Southern grande dame hoped her girls wouldn't grow up to be, but I was raised by a tribe of sexy Southern women who were predatory in their wealth of charms. When I first met Rosemary, she had just read from her first book of poems, **A Sexual Tour of the Deep South**. She had done a reading in a lecture hall in Callanwolde, sharing the stage with an excellent young poet named Coleman Barks. Later I would come to love the mystical, galvanic poetry of the Sufi dervish Rumi that Coleman translated with inordinate power. By soft light, my friend Bernie Schein and I listened to those two poets, Coleman and Rosemary, spewing words into the Atlanta darkness a block away from where I used to take the bus to kindergarten. In celebration of her own sexuality, Rosemary was a brand-new prototype of the Southern woman, the kind you were sure wouldn't tolerate the missionary position once she settled beneath the sheets.

At the writers' conference, Rosemary introduced me to each of the other women as old friends of hers, saving Alice Walker for last. Alice possessed a studied but queenly carriage. Wendy Weil was her agent in New York, and Wendy had shepherded me though all my inelegant stumbling through the New York literary world. Rosemary was protective and sisterly about Alice, so I thought we had enough in common to make us friends. Alice had been born and raised in Eatonton, Georgia, fifty miles away from the place she and I were standing when we shook hands. Her hand was as limp as an altar cloth.

"I read your book, and I really like it," I said as I handed her my copy of **Meridian.**

Alice Walker took the book, signed it, then returned it to me before turning away to open the back door of a nearby car. She had not spoken a single word to me. Her rudeness unnerved the other women with Rosemary.

"She has a thing about Southern white men, Pat," Rosemary explained.

"Sure seems to," I said.

Later, Rosemary Daniell would earn her own portion of wrath from Alice Walker. Though Rosemary was an early and articulate feminist, she riled the sisterhood with her groundbreaking book **Sleeping with Soldiers**. In it, Rosemary describes slumming on the wild side and sleeping with shrimpers, trailer trash, cowboys, tattooed soldiers, and anyone else she was attracted to on any given night. When I read it, I called Rosemary.

"Rosemary," I said. "Thank the good Lord in heaven that we never slept together."

I could tell I hurt her feelings when she responded, "I was good to my boys, Pat. No one's called to complain."

"It's not that, Rosemary," I said. "I'm thinking of what you might have written about me, something like, 'Conroy not only had chipmunk-size genitalia, he whined and cried like a baby when we had sex. Afterward he asked to try on my panty hose and Maidenform bra.' You're way too honest for me, kid."

"Honey, I bet we could've been famous in the sack. Famous!" Rosemary drawled.

Alice Walker's response to **Sleeping with Soldiers** was to write Rosemary a vituperative letter accusing her of a betrayal of the feminist movement and a celebration of the darkest forces of the sheer animalism of male sexuality. Walker considered the book a defacement and defilement of all that women had fought for in the twentieth century. Rosemary survived that dispiriting encounter with Alice

Walker, and she went on to establish a group for women whose voices have been heard around the world. The group is called Zona Rosa, and Rosemary travels all over the country to conduct workshops that change both the writings and the lives of women who cast their fate with this effervescent life force from Savannah, Georgia. I've spoken four times at Zona Rosa meetings, and I'm always invigorated by the powerful creative forces set loose when Rosemary and her group begin hurling ideas back and forth as though they were the shells of artillery fire. If forced to, I would say that Alice Walker was the better writer, but that Rosemary was the far better woman. In writing, in art, in everything, it always comes down to the condition of your own suffering, mortal heart. If my child were dying, I could put in a call to Rosemary and know she'd soon be in my house offering me words of comfort and bringing the spirit of Zona Rosa with her. But because she's Rosemary Daniell, she is mischievous, devil-may-care, unfathomable, and who knows what else that wild child might choose to do. At my first writers' conference, Rosemary burned like a new Southern flame while early success was in the process of butchering the kindly and commendable part of Alice Walker. She was as friendly as a cow turd on an altar step.

At the afternoon session the following day, I could barely contain my excitement over attending the poetry workshop of Adrienne Rich. She had won a National Book Award for her book **Diving into the Wreck,** which my sister Carol had recommended to me as both revolutionary and a work of art. In her all-star status, Rich had attracted the largest number of writers to her seminars, which were held in Callanwolde's cavernous main hall. Before the session began, Betsy Scott asked me to get everyone around us a cup of coffee to drink during Rich's lecture. Eight people stuck up their hands when I offered to make a coffee run to a rear kitchen on the other side of the mansion. I hurried off to get in line and return before things got started. A low hum of anticipation followed me as I took up position at the end of a long line and an inefficient team of coffee servers. Finally an attendant handed me my nine cups of coffee in a cardboard box loaded with packets of cream, Sweet'n Low, napkins, and spoons, and I began the slow, awkward balancing act back to the main hall.

The coffee cups in the thin box were lidless; hot coffee began spilling onto my wrists; and I almost tripped on an Oriental rug. A strange sound came from the lecture hall, both ominous and unsettling, but I couldn't lift my eyes from the shifting cups. When I got close enough, I could hear the angry hissing of the workshop participants. They sounded like an a cappella choir of rat snakes. It was not just sibilance I heard; it was hatred in a very undistilled form. It did not occur to me that the strident, S-shaped noise could be directed at me. Betsy Scott hurried up to me, frightened and obviously unsure as to what she should do. She took the box from me, laid it on the floor, and whispered, "Run, Pat. Get the hell out of here. They're hissing at you. At **you**. She kicked all the men out of her workshop—every one of them."

Looking up, I tried to take in the scene, get my bearings, and search for a route of escape all at once. Indeed, the hissing was meant for me alone. A hundred or so women were hissing at me as though I were some dormouse trying to crash a convention of feral cats. I sprinted toward a series of curtained portals that I thought were doors, but they turned out to be windows. I found myself flailing away at the window sashes and vermilion drapes and venetian blinds as the hissing grew louder behind me.

"This way, Pat!" Betsy yelled. "The door's all the way to the right."

She pulled me, and we were both running. When we reached the door, Betsy flung it open and pushed me through it as though I were the afternoon trash. Gasping for breath, I watched as a young man passed by me, heading toward the door Betsy held open that led to the forbidden hall. We watched this young man confront Adrienne Rich as she stood in regal attendance before her militant tribe. The hissing was as loud as a rookery of gannets while the angry young man faced down his detractors. Rich lifted a hand to silence them, and the man said, "I came to this conference because I love your poetry so much. I drove from Tampa, Florida. I brought all your books with me. This isn't right . . . what you've done. It will never be right. We're all Southerners here. We know what this is. Segregation. Nothing else. It's awful."

The great woman did not speak to him, but a cadre of her supporters surrounded him and eased him out of the hall toward where I watched the scene from the shadows. Betsy still held the doors open as the young man was pushed into the hallway next to me. It was not a violent moment, except that it was.

The other exiled men had gathered in a room on the second floor, and I found them to be a crestfallen group. John Stone and Gene Ellis, both Georgia poets, were among them, and my friend Cliff Graubart came over to greet me.

"Hey, Pat?" Cliff said. "When you didn't make it up here I thought those whacked-out chicks had killed you."

"It's not right," the man from Tampa repeated.

But the general mood of the men was one of broad-mindedness and resignation. John Stone summed it up best when he said, "Feminism is new. There're going to be a lot of stages it has to go through. Our job is to be patient. We're writers, so that's easy to do."

At the closing ceremony that night, I went to the poetry reading by Miller Williams. His was the last performance of the conference, but because of the chaos let loose by Adrienne Rich, the timetable of events got displaced. Miller Williams read his considerable poems to a smaller audience than he usually would expect. Though he was clearly exasperated by the events of the day, he was professional. He approached the podium and said, "This reading was supposed to have taken place two hours ago. I'm pleased that so many of you came back to hear my poetry. I'm happy to see that the young writer Pat Conroy came back for my reading. He thinks he's been anonymous this weekend, but David Madden and I both knew he was here. I loved his book **The Water Is Wide**. I dedicate this reading to you tonight, Mr. Conroy."

It was the first and last time a poet has dedicated a reading of poetry to me, and it stands as one of the great thrills of my career. Miller Williams's poetry moved and astonished me. I listened to him with an ardent pride when he read a poem at President Clinton's second inauguration in 1996.

In summing up my first writers' conference, I got insulted by Alice Walker, thrown out of a poetry workshop by Adrienne Rich, and had a poetry reading dedicated to me by Miller Williams. All in all, I thought I was in the middle of leading a grand and possibly even a fascinating life.

CHAPTER NINE

ON BEING A MILITARY BRAT

I was born and raised on federal property. America itself paid all the costs for my birth and my mother's long stay at the hospital. I was a military brat—one of America's children in the profoundest sense—and I was guaranteed free medical care and subsidized food and housing until the day I finished college and had to turn in the ID card that granted me these rights and privileges. The sound of gunfire on rifle ranges strikes an authentic chord of home in me even now. My father was a fighter pilot in the United States Marine Corps and fought for his country in three wars. I grew up invisibly in the aviator's house. We became quiet as bivalves at his approach and our lives were desperate and sad. But when the United States needed a fighter pilot, we did our best to provide one. Our contribution to the country was small, but so were we most of the time, and we gave all that we could.

I think being a military brat is one of the strangest and most interesting ways to spend an American childhood. The military brats of America are an invisible, unorganized tribe, a federation of brothers and sisters bound by common experience, by our uniformed fathers, by the movement of families being rotated through the American mainland and to military posts in foreign lands. We are an undiscovered nation living invisibly in the body politic of this country. There are millions of us scattered throughout America, but we have no special markings or passwords to identify one another when we move into a common field of vision. We grew up strangers to ourselves. We passed through our military childhoods unremembered. We were transients, billboards to be changed, body temperatures occupying school desks for a short time. We came and went like rented furniture, serviceable when you needed it, but unremarked upon after it was gone.

Who would have thought we were in the process of creating a brand-new culture in America? Several years ago, I discovered an extraordinary book called **Military Brats,** by Mary Edwards Wertsch. The book made me realize that military brats have done everything except tell our own stories. We've never stopped to honor ourselves, out loud, for our outstanding service to America. I come from a country that has no name, the one that Mary

Edwards Wertsch describes in her book. No Carolinian, no Georgian, has ever been as close to me and what I am in my blood than those military brats who lived out their childhoods going from base to base.

I was drafted into the Marine Corps on October 26, 1945, and I served the corps faithfully and proudly for twenty-one years. I moved more than twenty times and I attended eleven schools in twelve years. My job was to be a stranger, to know no one's name on the first day of school, to be ignorant of all history and flow and that familial sense of relationship and proportion that makes a town safe for a child.

By necessity, I made my own private treaty with rootlessness and spent my whole life trying to fake or invent a sense of place. **Home** is a foreign word in my vocabulary and always will be. At each new base and fresh assignment, I suffered through long months of trying to catch up and learning the steps required of those outsiders condemned to inhabit the airless margins of a child's world. My family drifted in and out of that archipelago of marine bases that begins with the Pentagon in Arlington, Virginia, and stretches down the coast to Parris Island in the South. I spent most of my childhood in North Carolina and few people in North Carolina know that salient fact. I've been claimed as native son by more than a few Southern states, but not by the one I spent the most time in as a child.

My mother, the loveliest of marine wives, always claimed to her seven children that we were in the middle of a wonderful, free-flowing life. Since it was the only life I'd ever lived, I had no choice but to believe her. She also provided me with the raw material for the protective shell I built for myself. As excuse or rationalization, it gave me comfort in the great solitude I was born into as a military brat. My mother explained that my loneliness was an act of patriotism. She knew how much the constant moving bothered me, but she convinced me that my country was somehow safer because my formidable, blue-eyed father practiced his deadly art at air stations around the South. We moved almost every year preparing for that existential moment ("This is no drill, son") when my violent father would take to the air against enemies fiercer than his wife or children.

That was a darker part of my service to my country. I grew up thinking my father would one day kill me. I never remember a time when I was not afraid of my father's hands except for those bright, palmy years when Dad was waging war or serving in carrier-based squadrons overseas. I used to pray that America would go to war or for Dad to get overseas assignments that would take him to Asian cities I'd never heard of. Ironically, a time of war for the United States became both respite and separate peace for my family. When my father was off killing the enemy, his family slept securely, and not because he was making the world safe for democracy.

Mom would not let us tell anyone that Dad was knocking us around. My silence was simply another facet of my patriotism. My youth filled up with the ancient shame of a son who cannot protect his mother. It would begin with an argument and the colonel's temper would rise (one did not argue with the colonel or the major or the captain or the lieutenant). He would backhand my mother, and her pitiful weeping would fill the room. Her seven children, quiet as Spartans, would lower their eyes and say nothing.

Later, my mother would recover and tell us that we had not seen what we had just seen. She turned us into unwitnesses of our own history. I breathed not a word of these troubling scenes to my teachers, coaches, relatives, or friends of the family. If asked, I think I'd have denied under torture that my father ever laid a hand on me. If the provost marshal had arrested my father for child abuse, his career in the Marine Corps would have ended at

that moment. So my mother took her beat-
ings and I took mine. My brothers and sisters, too, did their part for the corps. We did
not squeal and we earned our wings in our
father's dark and high-geared squadron.

To his dying day, my father always thought
I exaggerated the terror of my childhood.
I exaggerated nothing. Mine was a forced
march of blood and tears and I was always
afraid in my father's house. But I did it because I had no choice and because I was a
military brat conscripted at birth who had a
strong and unshakable sense of mission. I was
in the middle of a **long** and honorable service to my country, and part of that service
included letting my father practice the art of
warfare against me and the rest of the family.

The military life marked me out as one
of its own. I'm accustomed to order, to a
chain of command, to a list of rules at pool-
side, a spit-shined guard at the gate, retreat
at sunset, reveille at dawn, and everyone in
my world must be on time. Being late was
unimaginable in the world I grew up in, so I
always arrive at appointments early and find
it difficult to tolerate lateness in others. I always know what time it is even when I don't
carry a watch.

Because of the military life, I'm a stranger
everywhere and a stranger nowhere. I can en-

gage anyone in a conversation, become well liked in a matter of seconds, yet there is a distance I can never recover, a slight shiver of alienation, of not belonging, and an eye on the nearest door. The word "good-bye" will always be a killing thing to me, but so is the word "hello." I'm pathetic in my attempts to make friends with everyone I meet, from cabdrivers to bellhops to store clerks. When I was a child, my heart used to sink at every new move or new set of orders. By necessity, I became an expert at spotting outsiders. All through my youth, I was grateful for unpopular children. In their unhappiness, I saw my chance for rescue and I always leaped at it. When Mary Edwards Wertsch writes of military brats offering emotional blank checks to everyone in the world, she's writing the first line in my biography.

Yet I can walk away from best friends and rarely think of them again. I can close a door and not look back. There's something about my soul that's always ready to go, to break camp, to unfold the road map, to leave at night when the house inspection's done and the civilians are asleep and the open road is calling to the marine and his family again. I left twenty towns at night singing the Marine Corps hymn and it's that hymn that sets my blood on fire each time I hear it and takes me back to my ruined and magnificent childhood.

I brought so few gifts to the task of being a military brat. You learn who you are by testing and measuring yourself against the friends you grow up with. The military brat lacks those young, fixed critics who form opinions about your character over long, un-hurried years or who pass judgment on your behavior as your personality waxes and wanes during the insoluble dilemma that is child-hood. But I do know the raw artlessness of being an outsider.

Each year I began my life all over again. I grew up knowing no one well, least of all myself, and I think it damaged me. I grew up not knowing if I was smart or stupid, hand-some or ugly, interesting or insipid. I was too busy reacting to the changing landscapes and climates of my life to get any clear picture of myself. I was always leaving behind what I was just about ready to become. I could never catch up to the boy I might have been if I'd grown up in one place.

In 1972 my book **The Water Is Wide** came out when I was living in Beaufort, South Carolina. It was not the most popular book in South Carolina during that season, but it was extremely popular at the Marine Corps Air Station Beaufort, where the marines and their wives looked to me as a living affirmation of the military way of life. I accepted an invitation to speak at the Marine Corps officers' wives' club with the deep sense that some circle was being closed. Years before my mother had been an officer in the same club and she'd produced the first racially integrated program in the club's history. Neither of us knew that my speech would mark a turning point in both our lives.

Instead of talking about my new book and my experiences teaching on Daufuskie Island, I spoke of some things I wanted to say about the Marine Corps family. I was the son of a fighter pilot, as were a lot of their kids, and I had some things to tell them. I was the first military brat who'd ever spoken to the club—I was a native son. I could hear the inheld breath of these women as I approached the taboo subject of the kind of husbands and fathers I thought marines made. For the first time in my life I was hanging the laundry of my childhood out to dry. I told those women of the corps that I'd met many good soldiers in my life, but precious few good fathers. I also told them of my unbounded admiration for my mother and other military wives I'd met during my career as a brat. But I told those women directly that they shouldn't let their marines beat them or their children.

I thought I was giving a speech, but something astonishing was unleashed in that room that day. Some of the women present that day hated me, but some liked me very much. The response was electric, passionate, immediate. Some of the women approached me in tears, others in rage. But that talk to the officers' wives was the catalyst that first made me sit down and start writing the outline of **The Great Santini**.

A year later, the day after my father's retirement parade, my mother left my father after thirty-three years of marriage. Their divorce was ferocious and bitter, but it contained, miraculously, the seeds of my father's redemption. Alone and without the corps, he realized that his children were his enemies and that all seven of us thought he hated our guts. The American soldier is not taught to love his enemy or anyone else. Love did not come easily to my father, but he started trying to learn the steps after my mother left him. It was way too late for her, but his kids were ready for it. We'd been waiting all our lives for our dad to love us.

I had already begun the first chapters of **The Great Santini**. I wrote about a military brat who'd spent his whole life smiling and pretending that he was the happiest part of a perfect, indivisible American family. I had

no experience in writing down the graffiti left
along the margins of a boy's ruined heart. Because I was born a male, I had never wept for
the boy who'd once withstood the slaps and
blows of one of the corps' strongest aviators.
I'd never wept for my brothers or sisters or
my beautiful and loyal mother, yet I'd witnessed those brutal seasons of their fear and
hurt and sadness. Because I was born to be
a novelist, I remembered every scene, every
beating, every drop of blood shed by my
sweet and innocent family.

As I wrote, the child of the military in me
began to fall apart. For the one thing a military brat is not allowed to do is commit an
act of treason. I learned the hard way that
truth is a capital offense and so did my family. I created a boy named Ben Meecham and
I gave him my story. His loneliness, his unbearable solitude almost killed me as I wrote
about him. Everything about the boy hurt
me, but I kept writing the book because I
didn't know how to stop. My marriage would
fall apart and I'd spend several years trying to
figure out how not to be crazy because the
deep sadness of Ben Meecham and his family touched me with a pity I could not bear.
His father could love him only with his fists,
and I found myself inconsolable as I wrote
this. I would stare at pictures of myself taken

in high school and could not imagine why any father would want to hit that boy's face. I wrote **The Great Santini** through tears, hating everything my father stood for and sickened by his behavior toward his family.

But in the acknowledgment of this hatred, I also found myself composing a love song to my father and to the military way of life. Once when I read **Look Homeward, Angel** in high school, I'd lamented the fact that my father didn't have an interesting, artistic profession like Thomas Wolfe's stonecutter father. But in writing **Santini,** I realized that Thomas Wolfe's father never landed jets on aircraft carriers at night, wiped out a battalion of North Korean regulars crossing the Naktong River, or flew to Cuba with his squadron with the mission to clear the Cuban skies of MiGs if the flag went up.

In writing **The Great Santini** I had to consider the fact of my father's heroism. His job was extraordinarily dangerous and I never knew it. He never once complained about the perils of his vocation. He was one of those men who make the men of other nations pause before attacking America. I learned that I would not want to be an enemy soldier or tank when Don Conroy passed overhead. My father had made orphans out of many boys and girls in Asia during those years I prayed for God to make an orphan out of me. His job was to kill people when his nation asked him to, pure and simple. And the loving of his kids was never written into his job description.

When my mother left my father she found, to her great distress, that she was leaving the protective embrace of the corps she'd served for more than thirty years. She was shaken and disbelieving when a divorce court granted her five hundred dollars a month in child support but informed her she was not entitled to a dime of my dad's retirement pay. The court affirmed that it was the colonel who had served his country so valiantly, not she. But she'd been an exemplary wife of a marine officer and it was a career she had carried with rare grace and distinction. Peg Conroy made the whole Marine Corps a better place to be, but her career had a value of nothing when judged in a court of law. My mother died thinking that the Marine Corps had not done right by her. She had always considered herself and her children to be part of the grand design of the military, part of the mission.

There are no ceremonies to mark the end of our career as military brats, either. I imagined that all of us could meet on some impeccably manicured field, all the military brats, in a gathering so vast that it would be like the assembling of some vivid and undauntable army. We could come together on this parade ground at dusk, million-voiced and articulating our secret anthems of hurt and joy. We could praise one another in voices that understand both the magnificence and pain of our transient lives.

At the end of our assembly, we could pass in review in a parade of unutterable beauty. As brats, we've watched a thousand parades on a thousand weekends. We've shined shoes and polished brass and gotten every bedroom we ever slept in ready for Saturday morning inspection. A parade would be a piece of cake for the military brats of the world.

I would put all of our fathers in the reviewing stand, and require that they come in full dress uniform and in the prime of life. I want our fathers handsome and strong and feared by all the armies of the world the day they attend our parade.

To the ancient beat of drums we could pass by those erect and silent rows of fathers. What a fearful word "father" is to so many of us, but not on this day, when the marchers keep perfect step and the command for "eyes right" roars through our disciplined ranks and we turn to face our fathers in that crowd of warriors.

In this parade, these men would understand the nature and the value of their children's sacrifice for the first time. Our fathers
would stand at rigid attention. Then they
would begin to salute us, one by one, and in
that salute, that one sign of recognition, of
acknowledgment, they would thank us for
the first time. They would be thanking their
own children for their fortitude and courage
and generosity and long suffering, for endur-
ing a military childhood.

But most of all the salute would be for
something no military man in this country
has ever acknowledged. The gathering of
fighting men would be thanking their children, their fine and resourceful children, who
were strangers in every town they entered,
thanking them for their extraordinary service
to their country, for the sacrifices they made
over and over again to the United States of
America, to its ideals of freedom, to its pres-
ervation, and to its everlasting honor.

CHAPTER TEN

A SOUTHERNER IN PARIS

There are two women I would like to tell about my time in Paris and both of them are dead. It was the bright urgency of their high-spirited vitality, their heartfelt generous love of me as a boy, that led me to Paris in the first place.

There is Mary Vella, the Madame, the singularly exotic and beautiful French teacher at Beaufort High School who spoke French breathlessly, with a singing Carolina accent, with a dreaming, unpreservable quality. When she spoke to her class about Paris—her hair a thick aureole, a black crown; her complexion white and flowery; her figure full and Rubenesque—it was a distribution of gardenias from the human voice. The French language was an enchanting thing when spoken by the most romantic, offbeat figure in our innocent lives in those innocent times. After basketball games with the sweat still streaming from my body, she would kiss me and whisper, **"Très magnifique, monsieur."** She delivered her bouquets, her sweet compli-

ments, in the French language alone. Often Madame Vella would declare sadly that I was retarded in foreign languages, a verdict supported by my lackluster performance in the classroom. But, she said, my redemption would be the English language, and she told me she wanted to read a novel of mine after I had lived for a while in the City of Light, after I had walked the streets of Paris and learned the lessons only Paris could teach a writer. Madame Vella was radiant and magical and I missed her desperate quality, the gauzy, surreal loneliness veiled in the conjugation of French verbs. I missed the essential moment when French became her retreat, her gilded hermitage, the moment when her own language betrayed her. Finally, no language was powerful or humane enough to save her, and Mary Vella, impulsive and theatrical to her final breath, ended her life on Ribaut Road in Beaufort, South Carolina, with a single pistol shot through her brain. Hundreds of the monsieurs and mademoiselles who had populated her classes over the years gathered at the cemetery for her burial. It was like the death of the French language in the Carolina Low Country. When I finished writing **The Lords of Discipline** in Paris, I wanted to send Madame Vella the manuscript and tell her I had been true to her passionate urgings and had gone to Paris to write. But hers is one of those silent voices I sometimes hear when I enter the city of memory—her voice, seductive, immemorial, and clear, ordering me toward Paris.

The other woman is Ann Head, who was the lone writer in Beaufort when she taught me creative writing in 1963. She introduced me to French literature and led me to the journals of André Gide. With consummate grace, she criticized poems I wrote for her and never let me know that those poems were categorical, unimprovable violations of the very spirit of poetry. Once she confessed to me that she was not a good writer. I did not know what she meant then; I do now.

When I was a freshman in college, she sent me a copy of Hemingway's **A Moveable Feast** for my birthday and inscribed it, **One day I hope to read what you think about Paris. This is the best book I've ever read about the romance of writing.** She also told me to remember everything I could about my plebe year at The Citadel. She thought it would make a fine novel one day. She told me many things in her letters to me, things of extraordinary worth to a young writer, but she failed to tell me she would die of a brain hemorrhage years before I affirmed her generous belief in my gift.

It was the end of winter when I went to live in Paris, but the winter was a stubborn, long-winded one, and the bitter weather held firm until the end of April. The sky was gray in Paris for most of the spring and it rained almost every day. The city glistened beneath a remorseless, shimmering, mother-of-pearl sky. The people took their winter seriously, and whenever the sun would break through the clouds, the Luxembourg gardens would fill up with Parisians who would turn their pale, light-starved faces up toward the sun, like lizards. But in Paris during the spring of 1979, you mostly had the memory of what sunlight was like.

My task in Paris was to finish a novel— a novel I had partially written in Atlanta, in Charleston, and in two beach houses in South Carolina. It had become a habit of mine to write books in beautiful places, in rooms with exquisite views. Landscape and architecture affect the texture and quality of my prose; at least, that is the essential nature of my one grand superstition regarding the craft. For three years I had prepared myself for the final assault on this book. I had taken notes, conducted interviews, remembered hard, written down dialogues, filled journals, and prepared an extensive list of my weaknesses as a writer. Before I began to write in Paris, I reviewed these weaknesses: I was sentimental, often disastrously so; I was over-dramatic, showy with adjectives, safe with form, weak on verbs, overreliant on adverbs, confused banter with wit and dialogue, and could go on and on and on. . . . The flaws in my character were identical with the flaws in my prose, and I thought Paris would be good for both. When I stood on the Pont Neuf at the end of my first day in Paris and waved to a bargeman moving up the Seine against the current and watched the delicate silvering of the river at dusk, I felt there was no prose style Paris could not forgive.

There was a more practical reason for my residence in Paris during that time. My edi-tor, Jonathan Galassi, had taken a six-month leave of absence from Houghton Mifflin in order to translate the essays of Eugenio Mon-tale. Jonathan is a brilliant, articulate New Englander who looked as though he were the only offspring of a sexual liaison between Phillips Exeter and Sarah Lawrence. His edu-cational pedigree makes my own seem rather pallid and insubstantial. Boys from Beaufort High School and The Citadel avoid argu-ments with boys from Exeter and Harvard, with a bit of additional seasoning at Oxford. We try to wheedle them into fistfights in-stead. I had felt a moment of panic when I realized I had never heard of Montale, but lied with facility and claimed a long and intimate association with the Spanish poet. Jonathan informed me that Montale was Italian. Because I have an editor from Harvard, I go from one unbearable intellectual humiliation to another. But Jonathan encouraged me to come to Paris so we could write and work together. He and his wife, Susan, who was in Paris to write her dissertation on Picasso, helped me find a room on the top floor of the Grand Hôtel des Balcons in the sixth arrondissement. It was once the home of Hungarian lyric poet Endre Ady, whose epigram was engraved on the outside of the hotel: **Paris est plante en mon coeur**. It was one of the few sentences in French I could read without the help of a French–English dictionary. The concierge, a stout soldier of a woman, told me she was putting me on the top floor, which she reserved for "artistes." The next day, I spread my notes all over the room and began to write.

All writers are hostages of their own divine, unchangeable rituals. I am a prisoner of yellow legal pads and fountain pens. In habit lies safety. I like classical music playing softly in the background, and I carried a small transistor radio across the Atlantic to satisfy this harmless though fundamental need. But since the concierge had honored me with a residency on the sixth floor, I often had far more classical music than I desired. There was a flute player with the lung power of a small whale across the hall and an accordion player in the room next to mine. The accordion player, frail but absolutely indefatigable, would whack away at her indelicate instrument through much of the day. When the flute player practiced at the same time, the accordion player would become furious and there would be spirited disagreements between two-thirds of the artists in residence at the Grand Hôtel des Balcons. The concertos of accordion and flute made for a most obscene accompaniment.

I would turn the radio up loud, especially when the accordion lady began her daily assault against music. My room filled up with the sound of Mozart accompanied by accordion. By the end of the week I would rather have listened to a duet of tuba and spoons than listen to an accordion. I wanted to start a club to assassinate accordion players. When I memorized a long conciliatory French sentence and knocked on the accordion player's door to register a mild complaint about the noise, she howled demoniacally at me for ten minutes and played her accordion far into the night as an act of retribution for my temerity.

She was giving me my first memorable lesson into the nature of French national character and, more specifically, my first glimpse of that perverse and ornery creature, the Parisian.

Parisians and polar icecaps have a lot in common except that polar icecaps are warmer to strangers. There is something glacial, fishlike, and prodigiously remote about Parisians. At the sound of an approaching foreigner, their faces are as bland and expressionless as salamanders. When they fix you in their imperious stares, it is as if they are studying you from the raised periscopes of submarines right before they blow you out of the water. In Europe, climate shapes character, and the Parisians have been left out in the rain too long. But there is something irresistible in their sangfroid, magnificent in their imperturbability. Parisians also relish the xenophobic sport of stereotyping and love to offer an infinite variety of theories on the nature of Americans. To them, we as a people are shallow, criminally naïve, reactionary, decadent, over-the-hill, uncultured, uneducable, and friendly to a fault. To Parisians, all Americans are Texans, grinning cowboys. France is the only country in the world where friendliness is one of the seven deadly sins. I am deeply inoculated with the serum of American cheerfulness, and I had to make a serious effort to become melancholy and funereal in front of Parisians who called me "**frère**." To look Parisian, I walked around with my face tragically set as though I had just received a telegram announcing my mother's death. It was an admirable disguise, but my mouth betrayed me. Whenever Parisians heard my execrable attempts at French, they would cover their ears with their hands and moan over the violation and butchery of their sweet tongue. My concierge, with her great black autocratic slice of a face, grew increasingly indignant at my lack of facility in French. Her dark eyes, circled with bruised rings, would glower as she heard my voice skipping inexpertly through the dense arpeggios of her language. Finally, when her hostility had become a palpable, living thing at the Grand Hôtel des Balcons, I took her aside and, in a carefully memorized speech, confessed to her I was mentally retarded and had been sent to Paris on a special program of rehabilitation. With heartbreaking cries of, **"Oh, pardon, monsieur, pardon, pardon,"** she clutched me in a wrestler's grip to her breast. From that day forward, I received an extra croissant at breakfast, a maternal pat on the head, and she regarded each pitiful advance I made in the French language as miraculous and proof of a living God. Not only was I retarded, she would explain proudly to her friends, pointing her index finger to her temple, but I was also writing a book on the agonies of retardation on a grant from the American government.

I would work on the novel during the day, beginning at nine in the morning. I would break for lunch, walk down to the market street on the rue de Seine, buy food at the charcuterie, stop for a baguette, and bring the food back to my room. After lunch I would nap for an hour, rise, wash my face with cold water, then resume writing until five o'clock. There was an exceptional sameness to these days, a habitualness that pleased me immensely. I tried to fill up five legal pages a day, a quota that translated directly into seven typewritten, double-spaced pages. At the end of the first week I had twenty-eight pages. I worked seven days a week during the four months I lived in Paris, and before I left the Grand Hôtel des Balcons I would produce six hundred handwritten pages. It would be the most productive time in my life. I was living in Paris writing about Charleston, South Carolina, obsessed with the sharp beauty and all the prickly, mettlesome dilemmas of the Old South. By day I walked the old streets of Charleston, and by night I would walk the streets of Paris. Every evening I took long, unplanned walks through Paris, going in a different direction each time, trying to memorize and capture the immensity and hieratic radiance of the most beautiful city on earth. Each walk became a gathering of images stored like rare honey in the memory of my promenades through the city. There was the rue Mouffetard, the famous market street with its lush displays of mushrooms scrubbed and white as piano keys; bloodred tomatoes glistening in the rain; endives piled like the severed white ears of elves; wheels of Brie; the careful architecture of cheeses tiered dangerously high. There was the blood of horses on the butcher's apron in the **boucherie chevaline**; the stunned lambs' heads; hanging rabbits with fur left on their feet like socks; and pigs roasting whole on spits in the windows of Greek restaurants. Rue Mouffetard is a symphony of odors. You can close your eyes and describe with accuracy the shops you are passing. In the fish markets, there were the corpses of small eviscerated sharks staring outward toward the street; the trout arranged in rows like notes on a musical scale; prawns long as a man's hand; the eels split down the middle, hanging from ropes. Always there was a genius for display, order, and symmetry among French shopkeepers, a passion for the dignity of their trade.

There were the cathedrals that rose out of the city, immense buttressed tongues of stone, eloquent unimaginable canons of faith. Within those walls, the sun filtered through the stained-glass windows like lozenges of light through the tail feathers of peacocks. The windows were a celebration of sunlight. There was Notre Dame at night during a snowstorm with the flakes thickly swirling through the searchlights that illuminated the buttresses and gargoyles. The gargoyles, up close, through the snow, looked like the black dreams of God.

In the Luxembourg Gardens, there was an old woman who fed the birds with bread and seeds every evening at the same time. She had deep marks beneath her eyes like a pair of unmatched shoes. Her eyes had aged independently of each other and she walked with a cane. The birds and the woman rendezvoused at the same chair daily. She would put seeds in her mouth and the smallest, most courageous of the birds would hover about her face and kiss the seeds from her lips. The pigeons ruled the ground beneath her and would put the smaller birds to flight with rushing, bullying movements of their wings and chests. All around her was the small havoc of wings, the cries and secret language of birds, bread and seeds and wings and the sound of her laughter. When the food was gone, the birds would leave her, and the old woman in her blue coat would limp out of the park toward the rue de Vaugirard.

There were clochards of Paris—the winos, the dispossessed who lived beneath the bridges and in the metro stations. There were the injured, aggrieved men whom I would find sleeping on heated grates during rainstorms or throwing up on the benches of the metro stations. The vomit in the metro is always red, the color of table wine favored by the clochards. They are licensed by the city of Paris, and it must be a grim existential moment in a human life when you decide to register your name officially as a clochard.

There was a late-night walk when I came upon the bruised regiments of prostitutes on rue Saint-Denis who can proposition men in five or six languages. Some of the women were very beautiful; some were old, washed-out, desiccated. "I do anything you want, beeg boy," they would call out to me. "Don't be afraid, beeg boy. Brigitte be nice to beeg boy." And it would embarrass me that they unfailingly knew I was an American; I wore my nationality like a cheap cologne. In my imagination, syphilis bacilli, large as dogs, crouched in the dim vestibules and recesses of the disquieting street. In an Algerian district not far away, I witnessed fifty Algerian men bidding on a very young girl in the window. There was an auctioneer in the front of the window chiding the men for their cheapness, and the noise rose in pitch as the bidding grew feverish. The girl was very young, fragile, and she was not smiling. "It's her first time," my companion on the walk who spoke French said. "She's a virgin." The girl had a small birthmark on her cheek and was very pretty. I wondered about her most private, urgent thoughts at that moment before she stepped forth into the lewd demimonde of the twelfth arrondissement. I wondered how she felt about the eyes of men, of her childhood in France.

Walks through Paris, each night, each one different, each image a fragment, each fragment a bright sliver of memory always on call. It was always the same Paris and always a new Paris and I never tired of the walks. Walking along the Seine, stepping over the urine of clochards, smelling the perfume of the elegant fur-wrapped women emerging from La Tour d'Argent, peering into the high windows of the houses on the Île Saint-Louis, I could understand perfectly why the city of Paris had inspired so many artists for so many centuries. Such beauty and such decadence, in the old dance of life and lust and human sanctity in cities, creates a flammable desire to match such artistry. You want to prove yourself equal to such a city. In my walks through Paris I got to know the city and felt the first fledgling impulse to write about Paris; felt the old leap and stir as the images navigated the bloodstream, began to circulate in dreams and nightmares until they would one day burst forth as cries of the heart, psalms of the long season, poems of the exhausted flesh, and gargoyles. There is no writing, no art, without gargoyles.

It was no easy task to find a typist in Paris. Nor was it simple to find a typewriter with an American keyboard. I believed with all my innocent heart that all the keyboards of the Western world were identical. To my horror, the French keyboard looked as though it were assembled by the colicky Parisians whose hobby was playing the accordion. Typists are holy figures to me and I am both devotee and helot of their lightning-fingered craft. Normally I choose my typists with exquisite care, with the caution of the incurable paranoid, for the typist, no matter how discreet or devotional, becomes the writer's first critic. If you bore your typist, there is at least an outside chance that the world will sleep. I do not like my prose to be used as a nonaddictive substitute for Seconal. But, in Paris, I needed a typist with access to an American typewriter, so I could not exercise any choosiness. I placed an index card on a bulletin board at Shakespeare and Company and received not one inquiry. But one day in my second week—with the accordionist hacking away, the flutist piping, and my radio playing—I heard a furious argument break out down the hall, and it cheered my soul to hear two people screaming obscenities at each other in English. Later, I went down, knocked on the door, and met the man who would become my typist in Paris. He preferred the word "amanuensis." My amanuensis was named Mike and his girlfriend was called Dorea.

Mike needed money badly and he assured me he was an expert typist. He had worked his way through college typing term papers, won a coveted award for speed typing, and knew where a cheap American typewriter was for sale in a secondhand shop on the Right Bank. Mike, of course, had never typed a single phoneme in his life, but I would not learn this for several weeks. There was a superheroism, a ghastly brilliance, in Mike's unlimited capacity for lying. He was opinionated, high-strung, outrageous, one of those priestly fools of the open road you often encounter among young Americans backpacking through Europe. Dorea was quiet as a house-plant except when she was trading obsceni-ties with her love.

Two weeks later, when Mike brought me the first twenty pages of the typed manuscript, I wanted to sail Mike off the sixth floor like a Frisbee. I had never seen such inept typ-ing, much less paid money for it. But I had also rarely encountered a prevaricator of such remarkable gifts as this eloquent, half-crazed American.

"Mike," I yelled, "it looks like you typed this on a French keyboard! I like to have at least one or two words per page spelled right before I hand it to my editor. And each page looks like it's been painted with Wite-Out." I held up the first page, which was stiffened and disfigured with that strange liquid typists use to eradicate mistakes.

"There's a reason why the typing is so bad, Pat," Mike answered calmly. "It was because I was distracted by the brilliance of your prose."

"What?" I screamed again. "It's obvious you've never typed in your life."

"You're right. I confess it. I knew I couldn't fool you for long. You see too far into the spirit. My fingers actually trembled with pas-sion as I was swept away by the power of your prose. I couldn't sleep after I read your work.

Dorea will vouch for me, Pat. I looked up from the typewriter and said, 'Dorea, this man will see right through me. I can hide nothing from this man.'"

I said, "I have never met anyone so full of crap in my life."

"See, Dorea," Mike said, "he sees right through me."

"It's easy to spot a jerk," Dorea answered, dreamily blowing smoke out the window.

"I've been very distracted, Pat," Mike said, ignoring her. "But, of course, you already knew that."

"I didn't know that."

"Dorea has not had her period," Mike said.

"I'm sorry, but that doesn't have one thing to do with your lousy typing."

"Dorea has been indiscreet with another man," Mike admitted sadly. "It is not my child."

"I'm sorry," I whined, "but this is none of my business."

"I will marry Dorea anyway and raise the child as my own. I love her that much. But I know you have seen that already. I'm a slave to love."

"Fine," I said, wishing they would both leave, "but I didn't see that at all."

"I would also like to apologize for making that crack about Gertrude Stein when we

met the other day. I do not really hate homo-
sexuals. In fact, I am a reformed homosexual.
But, of course, with your insight, you knew
that already."

"It never even occurred to me."

"I was in a mental hospital long ago, but,
of course, you knew that. As an artist you
know everything about people."

"For some reason, Mike, that doesn't surprise me a bit."

"And I was on cocaine the day you hired
me to be your typist. Pat, I realize I am ob-
noxious and offend everyone—"

"Amen," Dorea whispered.

"—but I'm no longer crazy. I have come to
realize that it is the world that is insane, not
me. I was sick for my whole first month in
Paris but then I took a suppository. Americans are prejudiced against suppositories.
You should include that in your book. Dorea
has been sick for a week and won't take a
suppository. She prefers to be sick. But she
is pregnant and a suppository may help her
now. We are completely broke and we need
the money I'll make from typing your manuscript. Otherwise, the three of us will die of
starvation—Dorea, the baby, and me. But an
artist with your compassion would not let a
fetus die in the womb of such a fine woman."

Mike left my room that day with an advance for his services. He swore they would name the baby after me, even though I learned much later that Dorea was not pregnant. Within a month, after a vast expenditure for Wite-Out, I had trained an excellent typist and a trenchant literary critic to boot. I looked forward to Mike's visits, to his mad, pixilated, and subversive views of the world, and I kept a package of Gitanes for Dorea to smoke.

From travel I have observed that the Germans and the Japanese have inherited the earth. In the twentieth century, it was smart politics to be trounced soundly in a world war. Germans were ubiquitous that spring and the Japanese were the most passionate, untiring photographers on earth—they experienced the city of Paris through glass, through square apertures and focused lenses. I took eighteen photographs of Japanese couples on the Pont Royal as I crossed the Seine on the way to check my mail at the American Express office. The Japanese smile as frequently as Americans and their congenial politesse was as innate as their obsessive need to photograph. The Japanese and I dazzled one another with the white gunnery of our smiling. I like smiling nations and I learned to admire Japan as I checked my mail in Paris. A Japanese male without a camera looked undressed to me. They wore Nikons and Minoltas like monocles over their right eyes.

My first friend at the Grand Hôtel des Balcons was a twenty-two-year-old Japanese man whose passport was stolen in the metro, stranding him in Paris. His stay in Paris was a lonely one. At breakfast one morning, Mr. Hara smiled at me over his croissant, bowed formally, and said, "English velly bad."

"Japanese worse," I replied, pointing to myself.

"Velly sorry. Bad English," he said.

"Very sorry. Bad Japanese," I answered.

Mr. Hara had a shining, beautiful face, round as a melon, amber colored. "Speak velly well you, **français**."

"No **français**, no Japanese," I said.

"**Français** velly hard. I go to Japan soon. I sell Toyota. You know Toyota?"

"I drive a Datsun," I answered.

"Datsun velly bad. Toyota velly good."

Mr. Hara and I formed a rather unsteady alliance after this brief unsatisfactory encounter over breakfast. The language gulf was immense and unbridgeable but Mr. Hara was extremely lonely. He would come to my room each morning, bow deeply when I answered the door, and say with unimaginable formality that he would be very proud to have breakfast with me. He bought an

English–Japanese dictionary to help facilitate our exchanges. Mostly we grinned idiotically at each other, and I learned from conversing with Mr. Hara that it is as difficult to simplify your language as it is to increase its range. When he finally received a new passport, he invited me to lunch to celebrate his departure from France. Like all foreigners, Mr. Hara had suffered unpardonable indignities from French waiters. All French waiters seem like direct descendants of those hooded men who worked the guillotine for the Directory, and Mr. Hara held them all in bristling contempt. He had discovered a cafeteria in Saint-Germain-des-Prés without waiters, which was the only restaurant in Paris he would enter.

"I starve without this place," Mr. Hara said. "French velly bad. French hate Japanese people."

"The French hate everybody."

He toasted our friendship with a glass of red wine held aloft, then said to me, "Are you mad at Mr. Hara for Pearl Harbor?"

"No, of course not, Mr. Hara. Are you mad at me for Hiroshima?"

"Mr. Hara velly solly for Pearl Harbor. Velly solly for the Japanese people. Japan should have attacked France. That would be velly good."

"You don't mean that, Mr. Hara."

"Yes," he said fiercely, "then Mr. Hara would kill all French waiters. They hate Japanese people."

As we ate, Mr. Hara began reciting a list of atrocities committed against him in French restaurants. He talked and ate at the same time. He was not dexterous with a fork. He had ordered peas, and I do not think a single pea passed between his lips. There were peas on his shirt, sitting singly and in pairs on his arms, peas in his wine, peas spread across his side of the table, and peas rolling toward mine. When the peas were dispersed, he began dismembering his chicken breast with inelegant, skewering movements of his knife and fork. The chicken hit the floor twice, shooting off his plate like a flushed quail. He would pick it up, apologize, continue his bitter fulminations against the French nation, and beat at the chicken with his utensils. When the meal was done, I looked at Mr. Hara finishing his pea-flavored wine. When I saw his face, I could not keep from hooting. There were peas mashed on his chin, red cabbage hanging from the buttons of his shirt, chicken morsels on his upper lip. Remnants of his entire meal were scattered over his face and body. He laughed with me; then, staring at his fork, he declared, "Fork velly hard.

Chopsticks velly easy. The French invent fork? No, Mr. Pat?"

"I don't know, Mr. Hara."

"Yes. They invent fork. Because they hate Japanese people."

There would be other friends from the Grand Hôtel des Balcons; there would be Bill Koon playing his guitar and singing "Amanda" and his pretty girlfriend, Cindy, returning from the market with aromatic cheeses, duck pâté glazed with pepper, and bottles of red table wine; and Cathy Goldsmith, a woman from Toronto, who befriended the old chess players in the Luxembourg Gardens and each week brought me a fresh rose to bring me luck in my writing; and Margie Waller, a beautiful Fulbright scholar, who was finishing a book on Petrarch and writing an odd, brilliant paper comparing **Rebel Without a Cause** to **Star Wars;** and a stolid couple from the Yukon who described the migration of caribou near their cabin and the wolf packs that moved in concordance with the herds. There were friends for a day and friends for a week and we would meet at breakfast. I learned to carry a copy of the **International Herald Tribune** with me to breakfast as the testimonial emblem of my heritage. We exchanged information about Paris, about good cheap restaurants, about English-language book-

stores and the best places to exchange cur-
rency. Because we were strangers who would
know one another on this planet for a very
short time, we could trade those essential secrets of our lives that defined us in absolute
terms. Voyagers can remove the masks and
those sinuous, intricate disguises we wear at
home in the dangerous equilibrium of our
common lives. The men and women I met
at the Grand Hôtel des Balcons traveled to
change themselves, to trust their bright impulse with the hope they would receive the
gift of the sublime, life-changing encounter
somewhere on the road. There is no voyage
without a spiritual, even religious impulse.
Each of us had met by accident, our lives
touched briefly, fragilely—then we continued on our own private journeys, and those
intense encounters left a fragrant pollen on
the sills and eaves of memory. I could feel it;
it was mine. And those faces—pale, ethereal,
glowing dimly—are the coinage, the inexhaustible treasury, the winged golden bul-
lion of the voyage. Those faces, those friends
are the consecrated talismans of my leaving
home and living in the city of Paris.

Then there is the memory of food, of meals
eaten with Jonathan and Susan Galassi, the
wonderful cheap restaurants we discovered
by accident and design on the Left Bank.

There was Le Trumilou on the Seine, with its raw paintings, overlit dining room, its duck with prune sauce you could order for fifteen francs, its Sundays when the men from southern France sang folk songs from home and commanded silence from all the rest of us. There were Le Procope, Au Cochon de Lait, and Vagenende. Some Frenchmen bring their dogs to the restaurants with them, and often there was the sound of invisible dogs breaking discarded bones under a table. In the Café du Luxembourg, the proprietress owned a German shepherd who would lie against my feet as we ate dinner. There were memories of snails afloat in butter and garlic and parsley, oysters with the taste of Atlantic tides, mustards from Dijon, the flesh of sole flashing on a fork and lemon halves wrapped in gauze, sweetbreads swimming in thick cream flavored with paprika, prawns, and scallops, chicken breasts poached in Burgundy, marinated herring, rabbit pâté, and wines, splendid wines and cheap ones, wines of princes and wines of clochards, wines from Saint-Émilion and Brouilly and Bordeaux, from grapes ripened on hillsides the length and breadth of France. In Paris, it is a spiritual duty to grow fat.

In our finest meal, at Dodin-Bouffant, our one grandly extravagant Parisian meal, the waiter allowed us to taste a small portion of every dessert on the cart. There was the deep resonant taste of crème brûlée, small artillery explosions of flavor on the palate, all the black harmony of chocolate on the tongue, then the espresso, sharp and fierce, to wash it down. All the meals would be long and the conversations would continue over Armagnac, through nighttime walks in the rain, three of us under one umbrella, Jonathan and Susan in love, all of us in love, as we walked back to their hotel stepping carefully over the glistening cobblestones. Conversation with the Galassis was a splendid, unrecapturable thing; they were full-bodied, exhilarating, evanescent, and my mind would be blazing and overstimulated as I walked back to my hotel. When Jonathan and Susan left Paris for Rome, I did not think I could stand it. But we made plans to meet in Rome sometime in June. By then, I would have finished **The Lords of Discipline**. By then, my life in Paris would be over.

Also when I remember Paris, as I conjure the shimmering fragments of that river-praised, light-gifted city, it is not the walks through rain I remember most vividly, or the meals or the wine or the conversations. It is not even the writing, the creating of a world on paper, the hard labor of stillness or the quiet struggle to find the unassailably correct word, the startling and definitive image.

What I remember most is the explosions. I remember blood and shattered glass, fire and burning and death in the rain. I remember what I dream about, the nightmares I brought home to America, nightmares that passed unchallenged through customs, that evoked no official response. In the first explosion, I had no part to play except as a witness, as a helpless recorder of grief and desolation. In the second, fate refused to allow me the simple role of evangelist and storyteller, and handed me a major part, a lead role in a grisly dance of fire.

The first explosion occurred on March 26. I did not record the time. I was writing in the hotel, listening to the accordion music next door, and looking up a word in a new dictionary when there was a tremendous explosion somewhere near my hotel. I stepped out onto the balcony and saw the tuxedoed waiters from La Méditerranée sprinting in the direction of the Luxembourg Gardens. Racing downstairs, I joined the crowd that moved toward the rue de Vaugirard, where the traffic had stalled and people were screaming. There was smoke issuing from a small restau-

rant, Le Café Foyer, and broken glass everywhere. I passed by a pretty young woman
lying on a bench with her brown leather
boots primly crossed. A team of paramedics
was ministering to her. Her hair was black,
and she was wearing designer jeans. One of
her eyes was gone, and one of her ears blown
off. The blue lights of police cars flowered in
the mist. The explanation for the blast was
simple. Le Café Foyer was a Jewish restaurant
frequented by Jewish students from the Sorbonne. The Egyptian-Israeli pact had been
signed at Camp David in 1978, and the explosion was simply a form of protest, an edi-
torial of blood. A girl's ear blown off. Dead
kids drinking coffee. Because of history and
treaties, real estate and culture, I was watching a girl on a bench with her boots crossed
prettily, putting her hand up to the wound
where her eye used to be. But history was
meaningless to her now, and **Le Monde**
listed her among the dead in the next day's
paper. When I could not write for the next
several days, I tried to understand my relationship to the dying girl on the bench. Did I
have a responsibility to her? Of all the things
I saw that day, it is always the boots I see in
the nightmares—polished, serious boots. It is
one of the few things I know about her life.
She took excellent, almost obsessive care of

her boots. I know one other thing about her. She did not hear me when I shouted to her, "I'm so sorry." Nor did it occur to me to say it in French.

I finished **The Lords of Discipline** on May 18 at 12:30 p.m. It would take two weeks for Mike to complete typing the manuscript, and I had time to explore the Paris I had not seen, to entertain friends from Atlanta, to write letters, to work on my journal, and to buy souvenirs for my friends and three daughters. One of the souvenirs led me directly into the path of the second explosion.

My daughter Melissa, an incurable jock who beat up on other little girls in the DeKalb County soccer league, requested a simple gift from Paris: a soccer ball with the word "France" printed on it. On my last day in Paris I went searching for that soccer ball and finally found one in the sports section at the Galeries Lafayette. I checked my mail for a final time at the American Express office and left my Atlanta address in case any mail arrived after I left. I was leaving for Rome early the next morning and this was my day to bid farewell to a city that had been good to me. I walked through the Tuileries, past the Louvre, crossed the Seine, cut behind the Académie Française, and began walking up the rue de Seine. I had made this same walk twenty or thirty times since my arrival; I loved the small art galleries along both sides of the street and had visited most of them. I walked slowly, grateful that I had come to this city and had learned some things that would prove useful to me as a writer and a man. The final pages of the manuscript arrived, and I was taking the 960 pages to Jonathan in Rome. I had worked very hard and was feeling good about myself. I was halfway down the rue de Seine, moving dreamily, with no more words to write, emptied out, when there was an explosion ten feet in front of me. A wall of flame burst out of a small jewelry shop and climbed the wall of the shop directly across the street. I felt the heat of that enormous tongue of fire in my eyes, and my first thought was of terrorists. The second was of flight, and I pivoted back around toward the river and had taken the first step of what was going to be a very fast sprint when I heard a man screaming. I turned toward that scream, toward the last afternoon in Paris, toward my own small, insubstantial part in the history of the city, toward the dazzlement of human fate, and I saw a man on fire. The top of his head, his hair, his back, his arms and shoulders, his shirt were all on fire.

I have always wanted to be a man of courage. It has bothered me somewhat, but not much, that cowardice is a more frequent guest in my modest house of character. I like cowardice and enjoy the companionship and bonhomie of other cowards. I have seen quite enough of machismo in my life and consider myself one of its casualties. I prefer my friends to be cowards of the cringing, knock-kneed, fall-on-their-knees-and-beg variety, and they appreciate that same trembling quality in me. So it was with an absolute purity of terror that my first glance down the street confirmed the truth of what I already feared . . . I was the only one on the rue de Seine in any position to help.

I dropped the soccer ball in the middle of the street and chased after the man, who was beating at the flames with his hands, screaming and moving in a lurid, agonized dance across that narrow market street. He burst suddenly into the doorway of a store across the street with me right behind him, with me having absolutely no idea of what to do, with me praying for a single moment of valor. I tried to extinguish the flames with stinging, ineffectual slaps. Other people joined me and there was a shrill, immense pandemonium loose in that store as the smell of burning flesh entered our nostrils. Then I saw the curtains and I tell you those curtains came down from those windows, came down from those walls, came down from on high as I leaped on top of the burning man, covering his entire body as I took him to the floor rolling, rolling, rolling with this stranger in my arms. Feeling the wild beat of his heart, his muffled cries, his awesome panic, gripping him beneath the torn shrouds and rolling with him toward the door, I felt the most remarkable, grotesque intimacy. Then ten people must have landed on us. The rolling stopped and their weight hurt. Then we rose and I do not remember rising, but I remember people prying my arms from around the man swathed in ruined drapery. He was screaming and pushed me away when he saw it was me who was holding him, who was hurting him. We had extinguished the fire but there were puffed, terrible wounds where the fire had been. He pushed me again, then broke out of that circle of strangers and ran back into his burning store. He entered his store and tried to save his most valuable merchandise. I went after him, lifted him up from behind, hurt him once more, and carried him back to the street. He was in complete shock. He was one of two people in shock on the rue de Seine. He sat down on the curb and began moaning. His head and arms were wickedly burned, the gendarmes and the ambulances were arriving, and a huge crowd had gathered. "Is he all right?" I kept asking the crowd. Always in emergencies, my puny facility with the French language abandoned me. I had a single round burn on my elbow and the hair on the back of my hands and arms had been singed. I staggered away from the man when the gendarmes surrounded him in a protective cordon, felt the old familiar signs of migraine coming on, went to retrieve Melissa's soccer ball, and vomited in the middle of the rue de Seine.

I left the city of Paris the next day without knowing the fate of the burning man. On the way to Rome, I retraced my steps on that final day. If I had done things differently, stopped off for an espresso at a favorite café, lingered over my mail at the American Express office—there is a structure to accident and experience amazing in its complexity. I had walked into one of those rare, elemental moments of definition when I would be a different human being from what I was ever meant to be. I was destined to meet the burning man on rue de Seine and my whole life had been leading up to that moment. Coming to fire, moving toward grievous pain— toward my own vomit—with mail from my friends and a gift for my child. It had begun in high school because of a French teacher who would kill herself and a writer who would send me Hemingway's books about Paris. Then it was Proust, Balzac, Colette, Hugo, and a dozen others who put me on that street— those wonderful writers who would mark a young Southern boy with a passion for a city he knew only in words, in translation, a city he extravagantly loved and would one day write about. But none of those writers could tell me if the burning man had lived or died or what he meant to my life. In nightmares, I rolled and rolled again, felt the man's heart beating furiously beneath my palm, smelled the scalded oils of his flesh, and saw the boots of the Jewish girl murdered at Le Café Foyer.

I returned to Paris after **The Lords of Discipline** came out, and on the first day, I walked through the Luxembourg Gardens, visited the Grand Hôtel des Balcons, then walked down to the rue de Seine. I walked through the marketplace toward the river. I passed the vegetable stands, walked past the fishmongers, butchers, wine shops advertising Beaujoulais nouveau, past the flower shops toward the small **horlogerie** at 32 Rue de Seine. There was a light in the window of the shop, and it was snowing.

I looked in.

I saw the burning man repairing a watch and he looked up and saw me.

I nodded. He nodded back and had no

idea of our connection with each other. He had healed perfectly. I wanted to tell him who I was but I did not know how to begin. I wanted to kiss the head I had once seen on fire. What a strong and handsome man he was. I was numb with gratitude.

I talked about the burning man a lot. I am always trying to interpret the relationship between writing and life, between experience and art. Once I thought writing was a simple act, a matter of cataloging the most sacred items of God, the naming of things of darkness. But that definition was never good enough. It is not enough to name and catalog. But on my last day in Paris in 1979, I think, at last, I found the accurate figure of speech to describe the writing I wanted to do, found the relationship between life and art, and knew the things an artist must know. The burning man was my metaphor of art.

As a writer, I would have to walk many strange avenues, staying loose and keeping my eyes open, memorizing the names of streets and the faces of strangers, listening to unknown tongues, exploring severe, tended gardens, being aware of the traffic and the besieged faces pressed against windows in dimly lit houses. It was all in the moving and seeing, in the patience of voyaging, in a spiritual opening up to every experience, to every moment that touches the most sensitive cells of the soul's most private self. I could be a voyager in Atlanta as easily as in Paris, and if I was vigilant enough, if I paid attention to what I was doing and the books I wanted to write, I had discovered the duty and the central mystery of creation on the Rue de Seine on the Left Bank.

The writer must reach back deeply into memory, into those frightening unmarked streets, must walk until exhausted, eyes open, bearing gifts, mind blazing with the dignity of language, blood burning, images beginning to form like jade in the bloodstream. . . .

Until he turns that corner, reaches that street, arrives at that moment of pure divine inspiration, of ineffable chance, when there is an explosion—and he sees the burning man—then he can begin to write.

The burning man is always alive.

CHAPTER ELEVEN

A LOVE LETTER TO
THOMAS WOLFE

I have needed to write the American novelist Thomas Wolfe a love letter since I first
encountered him in Gene Norris's English
class at the end of 1961. Though I had no
way of knowing it then, I had entered into
the home territory of what would become
my literary terrain. For three months I had
been native to Beaufort, the year I believe I
came alive to myself as a human being, the
year I felt the fretful, uneasy awakening of
something rising within me that I could dis-
tinguish as belonging to me and me alone. It
marked the first time I could look into the
mirror and see that something was in there
staring back at me.

Gene Norris gave me a copy of **Look
Homeward, Angel** as a Christmas present
that December. **I think you are now ready
for the many pleasures of Thomas Wolfe,**
he wrote in the book, the first ever inscribed to
me. The book's impact on me was so visceral
that I mark the reading of **Look Homeward,
Angel** as one of the pivotal events of my

life. It starts off with the single greatest, knock-your-socks-off first page I have ever come across in my careful reading of world literature, and I consider myself a small-time aficionado of wonderful first and last pages. The book itself took full possession of me in a way no book has before or since. I read it from cover to cover three straight times, transfigured by the mesmerizing hold of the narrator's voice as I took in and fed on the power of the long line. It was the first time I realized that breathing and the written word were intimately connected to each other. I stepped into the bracing streams of Thomas Wolfe and could already hear the waterfalls forming in the cliffs that lay invisible beyond me. I kept holding my breath as I read **Look Homeward, Angel**. The beauty of the language, shaped in sentences as pretty as blue herons, brought me to my knees with pleasure. I did not know that words could pour through me like honey through a burst hive or that gardens seeded in dark secrecy could bloom along the borders of my half-ruined boyhood because a writer could touch me in all the broken places with his art.

During that Christmas, I was under the illusion that Thomas Wolfe had written his book solely because he knew that I would one day read it, that a boy in South Carolina would enter his house of art with his arms wide open, ready and waiting for everything that Thomas Wolfe could throw at him. The rhythms of his prose style, oceanic and brimming with strange life, infected the way I wrote and thought with an immovable virus I have never been able to shake. It is a well-known fact that I will carefully select four silvery, difficult-to-digest adjectives when one lean, Anglo-Saxon adjective will suffice. Once I entered into the country of Thomas Wolfe without visa or passport, I never went back to the boy I was before **Look Homeward, Angel**. Most flaws I have as a man and a writer I can trace directly to the early influence of Thomas Wolfe.

Wolfe's lunar sway over my writing so polluted the efforts of my high school and college years that they border on parody. I absorbed every bit of Wolfe's windiness and none of his specialness, his ecstatic singularity. I threw words all over the place and none of them landed right. For a full ten years, the estate of Thomas Wolfe could have sued me for plagiarism with perfect justification. My winds all howled and my rivers all roared out of the high hills, and my boys were all maddened and intoxicated with rich ores of both lust and loneliness, and my women were yolky with desire. Note the word "yolky." That is not Conroy. That is Thomas Wolfe. Before my complete submersion into the undertow of Wolfe's work, I wrote like any other normal American kid. After **Look Homeward, Angel** I wrote like a madman, a fool, and, many times, a nitwit. My love of Wolfe was passionate to the point of lunacy, and, I am afraid, somewhat hormonal in nature. He took my boyhood by storm. I burned and ached and hurt as I read and reread his books.

Mr. Norris was so concerned about Wolfe's effect on my writing that he gave me a second gift of a book when school was out the following summer. That book was Ernest Hemingway's **The Sun Also Rises**. But the gesture was futile. My course had been set inalterably and my prose was a floodplain for dizzying emanations from the snowy high slopes of a natural-born Wolfean. The cool, hard sentences of Hemingway were spare and shapely, but his sentences were trays of ice to me. I never could enroll in that it-is-true-and-good-and-spare-and-fine school of American writing. The language genie found itself stoppered and trapped in the bottle of my deepest self.

I began to call attention to myself. I could not help it. Thomas Wolfe had led me by the hand and introduced me to myself.

I read for fire. I have done so since the first day I read **Look Homeward, Angel**. Now, at last, I know what I was looking for then. I wanted to be lit up, all the cities and all the hill towns within me sacked and torn to the ground and the crops destroyed and the earth salted. Now, when I pick up a book, the prayer that rises out of me is that it changes me utterly and that I am not the man who first selected that book from a well-stocked shelf. Here's what I love: when a great writer turns me into a Jew from Chicago, a lesbian out of South Carolina, or a black woman moving into a subway entrance in Harlem. Turn me into something else, writers of the world. Make me Muslim, heretic, hermaphrodite. Put me into a crusader's armor, a cardinal's vestments. Let me feel the pygmy's heartbeat, the queen's breast, the torturer's pleasure, the Nile's taste, or the nomad's thirst. Tell me everything I must know. Hold nothing back.

I know of a thousand writers who are far better craftsmen than Thomas Wolfe. But few can bring a page to such astonishing life as Wolfe. Critics who do not like Wolfe often despise him, and his very name can induce nausea among the best of them. That is all right. They are just critics, and he is Thomas

Wolfe. In my wanderings about this country, I have never left a flower on the grave of a single critic, but I cannot count the number of roses I have left at Wolfe's grave in Asheville. I always save one for O. Henry, who is buried just down the hill.

Though I have said that my writing was influenced by Thomas Wolfe, that does not quite convey the religious nature of my humiliating devotion to his work. As a senior at Beaufort High School, I harangued a group of Mr. Norris's almost comatose juniors about the fevers and agues coaxed out of me by the sheer exhilaration of his writing. I throbbed, I writhed, I postured, I intoned, and I was perfectly ridiculous in every way. I cringe as I write to think about the droll figure I cut as the succubus of Thomas Wolfe's spirit took possession of me.

Here is the first poem I had published at The Citadel. Its title was "To Tom Wolf." It bothered me greatly that my editors had misspelled Wolfe and had shortened his name to Tom. But I was a plebe at The Citadel and one's editors were not particularly open to criticisms of their work by freshmen. The poem is painful for me to read now, but I would like you to know the completeness and the eagerness of my immersion into Wolfe's influence:

O sleep now, Tom, your pen is quelled.
You have a grave to show it.
But I have heard an eagle say
"These mountains need a poet."

I, of course, had never encountered an
eagle who said any such thing, or anything
at all. The poem wandered on for three more
queasy stanzas until it mercifully ended on
a bright, triumphant note of half-baked and
completely unearned ecstasy. Not a single
member of The Citadel community commented on my feverish ode to Thomas Wolfe,
although my mother considered it a work of
young, rough genius. It was a stone dropped
into The Citadel waters that made not a single
ripple. But my second poem, a bit of doggerel
I tossed off one night after a sweat party, gave
me my first taste of fame as an author and I
learned the invaluable lesson that fame could
be a killing thing, something I am not sure
that my literary hero, Thomas Wolfe, learned
in time. For several days, I became the most
famous poet in the history of The Citadel
when I published these four lines:

The dreams of youth are pleasant
    dreams,
Of women, vintage, and the sea.
Last night I dreamt I was a dog
Who found an upperclassman tree.

Upperclassmen from all four battalions were kind enough to visit me to discuss my poetry in depth. Not a single one asked me about Thomas Wolfe, but all expressed curiosity at my desire to urinate on them. They encouraged my passion for poetry by making me do push-ups until I dropped into a pool of my own vomit. My squad sergeant and I engaged in a brief, illuminating discussion of my theory of poetics. A man of few words, he made the eloquent gesture of urinating on my back while I was doing push-ups for him. I was barely eighteen, and as Thomas Wolfe had warned would be required of me, I had already suffered for my art.

My Wolfe fixation continued through my Citadel years and I delivered a paper on his writings to the Calliopean Literary Society in the spring of my senior year. My writing teacher, Captain C. F. Bargainnier, announced to my classmates that he would cheerfully shoot the teacher who had introduced me to the writing of Thomas Wolfe. My stories and poems all remained fiercely Wolfean in nature, if not stature. Many of my splendid professors at The Citadel tried to dam the rising tide of language as my prose began to strut its stuff in the throes of an uncontrollable delirium. They offered me a different path to knowledge and suggested that

I heed their gentle urging and concentrate on the elegance of simplicity. Simplicity, Herr Professors? Me? A Thomas Wolfe fanatic? A devotee? I did not listen to a single one of them, and my writing continued to set their teeth on edge.

When people do not like the writing of Thomas Wolfe, their dislike can assume a pure form of hatred. When Bernard DeVoto and Wright Morris attacked Wolfe's writing, they took a personal offense at his work and could not have been more brutally dismissive or insulting in their withering appraisal of his novels. Wolfe offends the sensibility of a certain kind of reader who prizes restraint, formality, a subtle and withholding eye, economy of style, and discretion of craft. There is nothing wrong with this species of reader, but it certainly leaves no room for appreciation of Wolfe's peculiar talent. If you love the couplet and the haiku, you might not be ready for the flood tides of Wolfe's oceanic magnitude. He demands that you must accede to richness and fullness and amplitude taken to their absolute extremes. Wolfe can do almost anything to the English language except hold back. His art is a shouted thing. He did not need a pulpit; Wolfe required a mountaintop so he could fling words like thunderbolts out toward the cold vestigial stars. He inhabits every line he writes and a little of Wolfe goes a long way for many readers. I know a novelist who believes Wolfe is the worst writer ever published in our republic, and he cannot think of whom he would put in second place.

I can turn to the first page of the first book, **Look Homeward, Angel,** that Thomas Wolfe published and give you examples of the two warring impulses always contained in his writing—both the good Thomas Wolfe, who can transfix a reader with an exuberant liveliness of style, and the bad Thomas Wolfe, whom critics ridicule for his windiness and the groping, hair-pulling abstractions he would turn to when trying to describe the unnameable, the very thing that tortured him, and, I think, tortures many of us. Among all the writers who ever lived, Wolfe provides the most fearless lesson plan in the dangers of trying to bring order out of chaos by putting down the unsayable thing. Though he gropes for exactitude, there are times when Wolfe is caught with his pants down, wallowing in a sinkhole of language. This exhausts some, offends others, nauseates many, and thrills me.

Wolfe's courage lay in the fact that he did not renounce that part of his work. He kept the howlings and incoherences and bawlings, these hymns of tongueless, inchoate madness that rise up in nightmare, in the moonless wastelands of sleep when the ores of greatness move through the soft cells of all artists, then disappear when the full light of day is upon us and we blush at the ravings and lunacies of our deepest selves. No one suffered more from the judgment of critics than Thomas Wolfe, yet he never once pulled back or tailored himself to fit the harshness of their theories.

I think he would have pulled his art together had he lived his full life as a writer. There are signs that he was beginning to gather the forces of his profligate talent when he died tragically, at thirty-seven years old, in Baltimore. I think the novels of his fifties and sixties would have been masterpieces. Time itself is a shaping, transfiguring force in any writer's life. Wolfe's best novels sleep in secret on a hillside in Asheville—beside him forever, or at least, this is what I believe.

Listen to the good Wolfe:

A destiny that leads the English to the Dutch is strange enough; but one that leads from Epsom into Pennsylvania, and thence into the hills that shut in Altamont over the proud coral cry of the cock, and the soft stone smile of an angel, is touched by that dark

miracle of chance which makes new
magic in a dusty world.
    Each of us is all the sums he
has not counted: subtract us into
nakedness and night again, and you
shall see begin in Crete four thousand
years ago the love that ended
yesterday in Texas.
    The seed of our destruction will
blossom in the desert, the alexin
of our cure grows by a mountain
rock, and our lives are haunted by a
Georgia slattern, because a London
cutpurse went unhung. Each moment
is the fruit of forty thousand years.
The minute-winning days, like
flies, buzz home to death, and every
moment is a window on all time.

This is imaginative narrative of a very high
order, gathered up by an intelligence as keen
and original as has ever appeared in American letters. When Wolfe wrote this page, his
was a singular and thrilling new voice out
to define a universe that looked different to
him than to anyone else. His prose style was
charged, poetic—each sentence a mule train
loaded with too much meaning and arid
beauty at the same time. It set Wolfe up for
both praise and mockery and both came at

him in a rush. As for me, I would cut off the top knuckle of my little finger to have written those words.

Yet, on the facing page of this splendid first page of his first book, Wolfe offers us a disembodied grouping of words, floating like some renegade constellation outside the range of any pull of gravity or control. Those of us who love him understand that he is always capable of breaking out in these uneasy anthems that scream the most intimate anguish of the troubled, desperado heart of a mountain boy.

Here is what the bad Wolfe sounds like, the writer who can send his most ardent critics backflipping out of their chairs:

> . . . a stone, a leaf, an unfound door; of a stone, a leaf, a door. And of all the forgotten faces.
>
> Naked and alone we came into exile. In her dark womb we did not know our mother's face; from the prison of her flesh have we come into the unspeakable and incommunicable prison of this earth.
>
> Which of us has known his brother? Which of us has looked into his father's heart? Which of us has not remained forever prison-pent? Which

of us is not forever a stranger and
alone?
    O waste of loss, in the hot mazes,
lost, among bright stars on this
most weary unbright cinder, lost!
Remembering speechlessly we seek
the great forgotten language, the lost
lane-end into heaven, a stone, a leaf,
an unfound door. Where? When?
    O lost, and by the wind grieved,
ghost, come back again.

Admittedly, this writing is not for everybody. He makes demands on the language
that seem to bring it to the breaking point.
Wolfe often gives you too much of too much
and then, just as you reach your interior point
of surrender, he gives you more. Quite possibly, his style can be the worst influence on a
young writer's life and work.

After my introduction to his work, I read
every book, every essay, every play, and every
letter that Wolfe ever wrote. I devoured—Ah!
there it is again. ("Devoured" is a pure Wolfean
word; he did not just eat, he devoured; he did
not just read a book, he devoured it. Wolfe
did not just enter a room, he devoured it and
everything inside it, gorged himself on every
image he encountered.) I became his acolyte
and his eternal flame and devoured the biog-

raphies that described his tortured peripatetic life and learned everything about him I could gather. Thomas Wolfe provided me with a blueprint on how even a boy like me could prepare myself to live a writer's life. By following the lead of this gargantuan, word-haunted man, I could force my way into a life of art. I was in the middle of a half-Southern boyhood, as lonely as an earthworm, moving with my family from base to base around the South with my mother standing in for the friends I never made. When I found out that Thomas Wolfe had died in 1938, I was almost inconsolable, for I had planned to find him and apprentice myself to him and clean his house and type his manuscripts and live my life to serve him. What the critics loathed most, I loved with all the clumsiness I brought to the task of being a boy. "He's not writing, idiots," I wanted to scream at them all. "Thomas Wolfe's not writing. Don't you see? Don't you understand? He's praying, you dumb sons of bitches. He's praying."

In my own writing, I return to my mother frequently because I keep discovering parts of her that she managed to hide from me when I was her worshipful child. I think it marvelous that she discussed her reading life with me, but from the beginning, her relationship with **Look Homeward, Angel** was different from her relationship with most other books. She and I regarded both the families Wolfe and Gant as extensions of our own. In depth, we discussed the various members of the Gant family and both of us were shocked when we discovered the literal nature of Wolfe's artistry after reading Elizabeth Nowell's biography (and yes, there is a stone, a leaf, and what I suppose to be an unfound door on the book's jacket). I longed to have a brother like Ben Gant and my mother could sympathize with W. O. Gant's raging tantrums because of my father's legendary temper. Like good students of literature, we began to make the comparisons and reach the conclusions that would both enrich and complicate our lives.

The book made areas accessible to us that had carried the impediment of taboo before. We began to talk more freely about my father's violence and how that family secret had exacted a price from us. It was Thomas Wolfe's father who opened that door of conversation in my hurt, traumatized family. I believed then, and still believe, that W. O. Wolfe was a violent man who beat his wife and his older sons. My mother totally disagreed and thought that Wolfe's father was a figure of high comedy. In my own time as a child, I took seriously the rampages of drunken men assaulting the peaceable kingdoms of sleeping families. The father in **Look Homeward, Angel** gave my mother and me an oblique way of approaching the one great forbidden subject that lay between us. It was the year of the last and most severe beating my father ever gave me, and the year I grew into my own body and into the young man strong enough to give pause even to the Great Santini. Because I could feel the overwhelming love that Wolfe experienced when he wrote about his maddening and outrageous father, he handed me the means to begin the long, excruciating process of learning how not to hate my own. Literature can do many things; sometimes it can even do the most important things.

The summer after my first encounter with Thomas Wolfe, Gene Norris proved that he was far more than just a great English teacher. He drove me to the boardinghouse in Asheville where Wolfe had grown up and that he had written about in **Look Homeward, Angel**. When I got out of the car, I realized that every step I took would be retracing the steps of Wolfe himself.

Mr. Norris walked me up the front stairs to the sitting porch and ordered me to sit in a rocking chair. Then he said, "The boarders would come out here after dinner to gossip and watch the sun go down."

I sat and rocked in a chair on the porch of the house where Thomas Wolfe had grown up, and I thought at that moment I was the happiest boy on earth.

A guide met us in the entry hall and showed us the great sitting room where the boarders would gather before dinner to listen to Mabel Wolfe play the piano and sing popular songs. The actual piano was there on display. The furniture was authentic and original, and the house still looked and felt like the place that Wolfe had written about. The dining room table was set for twenty-five or thirty people, and the china and silverware belonged to both the house and the book.

Memorabilia of Thomas Wolfe hung from the walls: photographs, drawings, diplomas, and samples of his handwriting laid out in display cases. Looking at Wolfe's handwriting came perilously close to being a religious experience for me. It satisfied some itch of recognition or acknowledgment I was unaware I even had. I saw his signature written at the bottom of a letter and understood for the first time the obsession of autograph collectors.

The guide led Mr. Norris and me into the small, cramped quarters off the kitchen where

Julia Wolfe lived out her days in heroic simplicity. The kitchen was large and functional, and the equipment displayed was exactly the same as it was when Mrs. Wolfe was feeding hungry tourists during the high season. Each room was exactly how Thomas Wolfe had described it. It was like being let loose in the pages of his novel.

When we walked upstairs, it was Gene Norris who led me to the bedroom in the far-right corner of the house, the most spacious of them all. Mr. Norris lightly touched my shoulder and said, "This is the room where Tom's brother Ben died. That's the bed where he died. In that chair, Mrs. Wolfe sat. His father sat over there. Tom watched his brother die from the foot of the bed."

My teacher knew that the death of Ben Gant in **Look Homeward, Angel** had torn me apart, tamed something in me with its chilling finality, and taught me something permanent and fine about an artist turning the worst moment of his life into something sweetly beautiful. When I read about the death of Ben Gant, I was certain I could feel as much pain as Thomas Wolfe, but I was uncertain whether I could love with such unflinching, astonishing power. I stared at that bed and those chairs and could not have felt more emotion if I had been brought to a bedroom made famous by the deaths of kings. That bed contained an aura of sanctity for me. The death of Ben Gant and the bed he died on had lived in my imagination, as vivid as fire itself, for six months before Gene Norris brought me face-to-face with them. I looked at the bed and saw the dying brother. The chairs held the mother, the father, and then the writer. I stared at the chair where Thomas Wolfe watched his brother die and I could barely contain my sorrow for the way the world cuts into us all by killing the softest of us first.

In the backyard, the apples were beginning to ripen on a tree, and the branches hung low, laden with bright fruit. The guide motioned for us to help ourselves, then said, "Thomas Wolfe used to love to eat the apples from this particular tree. He claimed the apples of western North Carolina were the best in the world."

Mr. Norris leaped up and grabbed an apple from a low-lying branch, gave it to me, and commanded, "Eat it, boy." As we drove out of Asheville and headed toward the road leading into the mountains and Lake Lure, I asked, "Why'd you want me to eat this apple, Mr. Norris?" Mr. Norris drove fast along the curves of the mountain road, pausing, selecting his words with care. "It's high time, boy, that you learned that there is a relationship between life and art."

So I learned it and ate that apple and remembered the words of my teacher. I set out to live my life and did it quite badly. One book had set me out in the direction that my soul was yearning to follow. Boys like me—you know the ones—we're the boys from the families no one knows, from schools that few have heard of, from towns defined by their own anonymity, from regions unpraised and unknown, from histories without stories or records or echoes or honor. Thomas Wolfe taught me that if I looked hard enough at the life I was living, the history of the world would play itself out before me within earshot of my mother's stove. I had to be vigilant, and courageous. But I already knew I was saddled with one great liability that could sabotage my career as a novelist from the outset.

"Mr. Norris?" I asked.

"Yes, creature," he answered.

"What a shame my parents are so boring," I said. "Thomas Wolfe had really interesting parents. His daddy was a stonecutter who carved angels for dead people. His mother owned a boardinghouse and became rich investing in land. My old man's a jarhead. Mom's just a housewife."

Mr. Norris shot me one of his most disapproving glances. "Your father's checked out to carry nuclear weapons against our nation's enemies, boy. He breaks the sound barrier when he goes to work every day. You looked at your mother lately? Beauty, brains—Peg could be the president of General Motors, not raising critters sorry as you."

With that second burst of great teaching that day, Gene Norris set me on the road that would lead to my life's work. I began to study my parents the way a lepidopterist pored over the details of a luna moth's wing structure. They sprang to bewildering, amazing life to me under my secret inspection of every aspect of their lives.

The following October, my mother drove me out to the Marine Corps Air Station Beaufort in morning darkness. We watched as my father and his squadron scrambled off the runway on the way to Roosevelt Roads in Puerto Rico. The Cuban Missile Crisis was heating up and Russian ships on the high seas were shipping nuclear warheads into Cuba. My father and his men were part of the American forces that would stop them if war was declared. I was afraid for the whole world. My mother said the rosary, quietly and to herself, until I asked, "Mama, are you praying for Dad and his pilots?"

"No, son," Peg Conroy answered, wife of

a marine fighter pilot, helpmeet of an American warrior. She prayed as the planes rose in thunderous noise around us and said, "I'm praying for the souls of the Cuban pilots your father and his men are going to kill."

I stared at my mother as though I had never seen her before. I knew her as carpooler, housewife, party girl, terrific dancer, beachcomber, president of the PTA, and a hundred other disguises she used to hide herself from me. My mother revealed her true identity at last and let me know that I was sitting in a Chevrolet station wagon next to a goddess of battle.

When Dad returned home disappointed that the Russian navy had turned back and the flag had not gone up, I got up my nerve to ask him about the things he saw and felt training his squadron for war above the skies of the Caribbean.

"Dad, what was your mission in Cuba? If war had broken out?" I asked.

"You a detective, jocko?" he asked.

"No, sir. I was just curious."

He looked at me, then said, "To clear the air of MiGs over Cuba."

"You think you could have done it?" I asked.

My father stared me down, then answered in the voice of the Great Santini, "There wouldn't have been a bluebird flying over that island, son."

Look Homeward, Angel was the text of my liberation into myself, the one that gave me access to the ceremonies and procedures that could lead me to the writer's way. Because Thomas Wolfe had done me the immense favor of dying, I could study his life and career from beginning to end and try to learn by his example and guard against his mistakes. Because he seemed to be much like me—no, that is dishonest. What I meant to say and was afraid to say is that I thought that Thomas Wolfe **was** me. My identification with this one extravagantly American and exaggeratedly Southern writer was so complete as to border on the demented and the mystical. His life has long served as the ox goad to the passion and inflammation I bring to all discussions of art.

It has become almost a rite of passage for Southern male writers of great talent to take their turns deflating the literary reputation of Thomas Wolfe. Academics, with some rare exceptions, have been murderous in their appraisal of the merits and quality of Wolfe's work. He inspires more mockery than devotion. English professors in major universities attach the names of other writers to their résumés if they want either tenure or publication. Wolfe's reputation seems to dim year by year, and academics cannot quite forgive him for the absolute temerity of his daring to write like Thomas Wolfe and not someone much better.

I, however, stand by my absolute devotion to the man and his work. Do I not see his flaws? Of course I do, but I see my own with much greater sadness and embarrassment. Has my taste in literature not grown and matured and become far more refined than it was when I was a boy? I certainly hope so, but here is why I still pull guard duty for Thomas Wolfe: I think that he tells more of the truth about the world he found himself in than anyone else has. Anyone. Wolfe hovers above a blank page like God dreaming of paradise. With every word he writes he tries to give you a complete and autonomous world. Because he cannot do otherwise, Wolfe takes you high up into the mountains, past the tree line, to those crests and snowy peaks of the highest points of the earth. He stammers, he murmurs, he hunts for the right words, and words spill out of his pockets and cuffs and shirtsleeves as he tries to awaken us from the dream of our own barely lived-in lives. When he spots our interest flagging, he flails his arms, collars us, makes us look upward out toward the stars where all the mysteries and silences and functions and secrets of time are. Thomas Wolfe tries to tell you things that none of us are supposed to know. His art fails because he cannot quite deliver the goods and the critics know it. This does not stop him because Wolfe knows that he is onto something very big. He almost gets it . . . he almost takes us there . . . he almost pulls it off and that's why those who love his work revere him. Wolfe writes like a man on fire who does not have a clue how not to be on fire. Yes, I see the flaws of Thomas Wolfe and I could not care less. His art is overdone and yet I find it incomparably beautiful. I still honor the boy who accepted Thomas Wolfe into his life when he was sixteen. I do not know what I would have done if he had failed to find me that year in Gene Norris's English class or where I would be or what I would be doing. I owe my life as an artist to him, and I will never forget that debt or dismiss his work with my scorn. I thank him with my heart for the greatness of his spirit and work.

CHAPTER TWELVE

THE COUNT

Many writers and critics have called Leo Tolstoy's magisterial novel **War and Peace** the greatest novel ever written, and their ranks include such luminaries as E. M. Forster, John Galsworthy, and Hugh Walpole. Virginia Woolf gushed over it like a schoolgirl, saying, "If . . . you think of the novels which seem to you great novels—**War and Peace, Vanity Fair, Tristram Shandy, Madame Bovary, Pride and Prejudice, The Mayor of Casterbridge, Villette**—if you think of these books, you do at once think about some character who has seemed to you so real (I do not by that mean so lifelike) that it has the power to make you think not merely of it itself, but all sorts of things through its eyes—of religion, of love, of war, of peace, of family life, of balls in country towns, of sunsets, moonrises, the immortality of the soul. There is hardly any subject of human experience that is left out of **War and Peace. . . .**"

Let me now add my own voice to the hallelujah chorus of novelists who have found

themselves enraptured by the immensity and luminosity of **War and Peace** and cast my own vote that it is the finest novel ever written. I can think of no other novelist who could take the entire known world as his subject matter and not be overwhelmed by the task at hand. But Count Leo Tolstoy writes with such assuredness and unshowy mastery that his powers can sometimes strike you as almost godlike as he looks over the world of the Napoleonic Wars with the calmness and certainty of a master surveying a chessboard with a hundred thousand pieces. Tolstoy overwhelms and humbles and delights me. He is massively interested in everything he sees around him. Nothing escapes his attention, and there does not seem to be a single subject that bores him. His subject is all the world and all the people and creatures who populate it and everything in between. Once you plunge into the inexhaustible depths of **War and Peace,** Count Tolstoy will take you prisoner for more than thirteen hundred pages. He will exhaust you with the deadly movement of troops the length and breadth of Europe; dance with you at soirees where you meet some of the most fascinating people in literature; make you happy to be young, fearful to be old, eager for battle, terrified of battle, anxious to fall in love, be-

264 || PAT CONROY

trayed by the deepest soundings of love; place you in the middle of conversations with serfs and in the company of tsars—Tolstoy will do everything a novelist can do with all the magnanimity and confidence one possesses when one is born to be the greatest novelist who ever lived.

When I first bought **War and Peace,** I was showing off to my splendid English teacher at Gonzaga High School, Joseph Monte, who had handed out a list of a hundred great books that we should read before leaving home for college. The sheer size of the book both intimidated and spurred me on to begin reading it as quickly as I could. It was my announcement to myself that I was going to be a serious student of literature for the rest of my life. For a year, Mr. Monte had taught me that I wanted to be smart and gifted in the language more than anything else. I read **David Copperfield** and **The Peloponnesian War** and **The Sound and the Fury** and **Crime and Punishment** under the wondrous scrutiny of his tutelage. When I bought my copy of **War and Peace,** Mr. Monte simply nodded in approval, as though I had taken my first step on a newly discovered continent.

When I booked a return flight on **War and Peace,** I was in my thirties and had made my living writing novels for a good ten years. But

I felt seized by an overwhelming urge to seek a deeper knowledge of and a mastery of my craft that writing books alone had failed to grant me. I wanted to read **War and Peace** as a mature and, I hoped, discerning man, and I wanted to take my time doing it, so I could study its labyrinthine architecture to see how its great engines worked. On my second around-the-world voyage with this novel, I took thorough notes and made charts of battles and wrote down family trees and tried to plunder the riches of Tolstoy's art, in much the same way the French army had fleeced the abandoned mansions of Moscow after the Russian army had pulled back from the city. I studied battle maps of Austerlitz and Borodino and read accounts of Napoleon's life and the court life of the Russian aristocracy at the time of the French invasion. It was at this time that I studied biographies of Tolstoy and began reading about friends and relatives of the count who he placed in key fictional roles throughout his voluminous novel. I tried to understand its matchlessness, the perfection of its grandeur, its intimidating lucidity, and the unsurpassable authority of its narrative power. My amazement was in its naturalness, as though it poured out of Tolstoy's soul in a pure stream of light. There was no strain or sign of heavy lifting in Tolstoy until he arrives at his onerous but pardonable theories of history, which struck me on the second reading as didactic. If I am honest with myself, I think I skipped over all his historical musings the first time I read the book because I was so anxious about the fate of characters I had come to know and love. I cared deeply about their stories as the armies of Napoleon crossed the Niemen River, entering the heart of Mother Russia and affecting the life of every character in the book.

On the third reading, I found that spending time between the pages of **War and Peace** was one of the most compensatory pursuits I had ever discovered. I cannot think of another novelist who writes with such serene self-confidence. As a narrator, Tolstoy creates a world that seems miraculous in its inclusiveness and its nobility of effect and even its strange lightness on its feet. You feel everything in **War and Peace** except the strain of its creation. It's like a book made from starlight and fire; the spirit of life itself lends it structure. The language is always in sublime service to the force of this light that illuminates the entire work. On my third reading, I even read Tolstoy's discourses on history with great pleasure.

The novel begins without fanfare or introduction at Anna Pavlovna Scherer's soiree in St. Petersburg. She is speaking with a fierceness that tells us a truth about the forces that will drive the entire book. "**Eh bien, mon prince,**" she begins. With great irritation and contempt, Anna tells Prince Vasili Kuragin she understands that the kingdoms of both Genoa and Lucca in Italy are now family estates of the Bonapartes. In her second sentence, she warns the prince that if he even tries to defend the horror and infamies of Napoleon, whom she refers to twice as the Antichrist, then she will terminate their friendship, and she will no longer function as the prince's "faithful slave." Thus, the novel is laid out in its introductory speech delivered by a voice that sounds like Mother Russia herself. Tolstoy catapults us into the center of the aristocratic life of Russia's most sophisticated society at a party that has continued to attract millions of readers since the book's publication in 1869. In its completeness and almost eerie circularity, the speech of Anna Pavlovna could just as appropriately serve as the last words of the book.

The conversations at this party are carried off with such artfulness and authority it makes dinner parties I have attended in New York City and Los Angeles seem like they were conducted by the barely living for the recently dead. This party hums with bright intellect and a lust for living that is as fresh today as it was when first written. The reader finds the spontaneous nexus of the Tolstoyan genius on the first page as he informs us that Anna Pavlovna's invitations have been written in her own hand—in French—and that she refers to her slight cough as "**la grippe,**" which has become fashionable among the elite in St. Petersburg society that season. Tolstoy's details always seem to shimmer with a delicacy of precision.

In his supreme naturalness, Tolstoy introduces two of the most important characters of this novel at the same party: the stout, nearsighted Pierre, the illegitimate son of Count Cyril Bezukhov, a fabulously wealthy nobleman whose youth dated from the time of Catherine the Great. In his shambling, good-natured innocence, Pierre will become the conscience and the lodestar of the story, and his charming affability and deep intellectual curiosity will make his arrival on any scene or battlefield a welcome one. Pierre's social clumsiness displays itself immediately when he defends Napoleon as a principled defender of the rights of man and the equality of all people, in front of the horrified Anna Pavlovna and a roomful of guests who owe their quality of life to the institution of serfdom. Only Prince Andrei Bolkonsky smiles at Pierre's naïveté, since he and Pierre are already devoted friends, as we will discover in the next chapter. Prince Andrei is the next most important man in the narrative, as well as one of the most stalwart and admirable characters in world fiction. Biographies have argued persuasively that Pierre and Andrei represent two partitions of Leo Tolstoy's world-encompassing personality. If this is true, Tolstoy was a fascinating, complicated, and self-actualized man. He is the kind of writer who wants and needs readers to fall in love with his characters, and this novel will make you dizzy with a joyous affection for the people you will meet on these pages. I fell in love with Natasha Rostova when I was a teenage boy and let it happen again after my third reading of this inexhaustible novel at the age of sixty-one. Tolstoy would find my attraction to Natasha a natural response, for he is, at the dead center of his art, a great nature writer, and nothing is more natural in his world than the mysterious and necessary attraction of men and women. It is impossible not to be suffused with happiness when Prince Andrei and Natasha announce their love for each other. Their impending marriage seems part of the design of the universe, as right as the stars that make up the belt of Orion.

Nor can we feel anything but despair when Natasha becomes infatuated with the dashing, insincere scoundrel Anatole Kuragin, who steals her affections when Andrei disappears from her life while recuperating from wounds that almost killed him on the fields at Austerlitz. Kuragin offers convincing proof that Tolstoy also studied and understood the slackest and most corrosive instincts of mankind. Kuragin's thoughtless villainy can still be found in any American fraternity house today. How many times in human history has the most exquisite girl in a city fallen for an unsavory man unworthy of her delectable charms? It has remained a classic theme of world literature since Eve listened to the entreaties of the serpent in the Garden of Eden, and it continues to be a staple of both life and fiction in the present day. It is Tolstoy's uncanny brilliance as an artist that Natasha's betrayal of Prince Andrei causes the reader anguish, but I would wager that it also broke Tolstoy's heart to write that scene. You feel the presiding majesty of the author on every page even as he takes great pains to conceal himself.

Later, the compassion and humanity of the novelist assert themselves, and Tolstoy allows Natasha to redeem herself after Moscow has fallen into the hands of the French and the Rostov family is fleeing the burning city. Natasha discovers that one of the wagons in the flight from Moscow is carrying the mortally wounded Prince Andrei. The lovers are reconciled before Prince Andrei's inevitable, unspeakable death. Tolstoy watches over the death of Prince Andrei with restraint and a harmonic dignity, and resorts to no histrionics or the use of a single writerly trick to make the prince's death more dramatic or tragic. Three times in my life I have read about the death of Prince Andrei, and three times I have wept uncontrollably. "Uncontrollably" is not a word that Leo Tolstoy would use. But I am not Leo Tolstoy, and I want it known that I wept, which is my description of how it felt to lose this wonderful man still another time in my lifetime of devouring the great books.

In **War and Peace,** we follow the destinies of five families as their lives are ripped asunder by the Napoleonic Wars. We attend stuffy balls in swank, sophisticated St. Petersburg with the Kuragins and the Drubetskoys where snobbishness is an art form and the workings of the court a quiet war of maneuvering and attrition. In Moscow, Tolstoy introduces us to the simpler pleasures of the Rostov family, who celebrate the name day of the two Natashas, mother and daughter. Moscow is more down-to-earth and a less self-conscious city than St. Petersburg. Tolstoy lets us in on this valuable secret because the aristocracy speaks Russian, not French, in Moscow. Later, we will travel to Bald Hills to meet Andrei's formidable father, Prince Nikolai Bolkonsky, and his sister, Maria, in a country estate that sounds much like the one Tolstoy presided over at Yasnaya Polyana, a little over 124 miles southwest of Moscow that almost lay on a direct route of the French army.

There is a calmness in presentation every time Tolstoy introduces us to a new character or setting. He takes no shortcuts or back roads, and there is not a single hurried line in the book. When he describes a new character, he does it with economy and concision, but absolutely no haste. The dialogue he places in the mouths of these characters illuminates their qualities with a perfection that is dazzling. The speaking voice of Andrei could never be mistaken for that of Pierre. Natasha's distinctive voice could never lead you to believe it is Princess Maria speaking; their voices are individual, recognizable, and pitch-perfect. The language of Leo Tolstoy will seldom amaze you. He is not the kind of writer who makes you breathless with his hijinks or fancy footwork in the hothouse kingdom of words. Not a single time do you have to struggle to understand what he is saying or what he is trying to convey to you. There has never been a writer of his mastery who wrote with such clarity and ease. Never does he want to confuse or neglect you. When he takes you on a wolf hunt, you will know exactly how it feels to be on horseback in the pursuit of a wolf in the middle of Russia. If you accompany him to the battlefield of Borodino, you will know precisely how it felt to be a Russian general, an artillery officer, a rifleman on the front lines, a French drummer boy, a cavalry officer, or Pierre watching the battle from the knoll at Gorky. If Tolstoy takes you to a dance in Moscow, he will teach you how to act, and you get the feeling he would actually like to teach you how to dance. When Moscow burns, he makes you feel the heat of the fires, the chaos in the burning city, the greed on the faces of the looters, and the terror of a pretty but unnamed Armenian girl fearful about being raped by the rampaging French soldiers. Tolstoy can make you feel anything he wants you to feel, and his artfulness is of such a high order, you are unaware of his doing it. Though it seems impossible to me, Tolstoy writes about women as well as he does about the world and affairs of men. I think he writes about women as well as any of the great women novelists, such as

Jane Austen or George Eliot, whose works I revere. He is as comfortable with women gossiping in a boudoir as he is describing the loading and firing of cannons by artillerymen at the Battle of Austerlitz. In the dispensation of the talents given to a novelist, Tolstoy seems to have gotten it all, equipped with every weapon in the arsenal. His sentences seem to spring out of the Russian earth. You cannot read **War and Peace** and not pause before launching an attack on a country that produces men such as Leo Tolstoy.

As a graduate of The Citadel, I am astonished by Tolstoy's absolute mastery at describing battles and military tactics. If I were teaching military history in any country in the world, I would make **War and Peace** required reading for anyone who held any ambition for advancement into the officer corps. It should be on the night table of the leader of every country who wishes to send troops into war. No writer has ever described the horror and anarchy of battle with more authority. It is one of the timeless lessons of **War and Peace** that no one—not Napoleon, nor the tsar, nor the Russian general Kutuzov—has any idea how a war is going to turn out once it is unleashed. Napoleon died believing that his French armies won the Battle of Borodino, yet Tolstoy is completely convincing when he states that this bloody and unnecessary battle marked the beginning of the dissolution of the Napoleonic era. It is Tolstoy's strongly held conviction that no man knows the forces that may be set loose when an army enters the homeland of a proud enemy whose people speak a different language, dance to a different music, worship a sterner god, and do not take well to an invasion of the motherland by an arrogant enemy. If I have one certainty in the world, it is that Adolf Hitler did not read **War and Peace** before he sent the armies of the Third Reich into the heart of Russia. Leo Tolstoy had already written the outcome of that nightmarish scenario when this novel was published in 1869. It makes me wonder if Lyndon Johnson had read **War and Peace** before he escalated the Vietnam War after the Gulf of Tonkin Incident, or if George W. Bush had paid the book some attention before the invasion of Iraq. Tolstoy does not provide all the answers to the problems of modern warfare, but he certainly can help you grasp some of the essential questions you should ask yourself before sending your soldiers across a border that is not your own. I think that **War and Peace** is the best book about war ever written, and that includes **The Iliad**. It is also the best book about peace ever written. Over the years, many critics have said that **War and Peace** is not even a novel, and they may be right. Whatever it is, there has never been anything close to touching it. It stands alone. A star in the east. Magnificent. One of a kind. It can be praised by the most sublime word in the language—it is Tolstoyan, worthy of the tortured, fabulous Russian Count Leo Tolstoy.

I envy the young man or woman picking up this book for the first time more than any reader in the world. Our own great Henry James thought Tolstoy lacked craftsmanship, but I think the great Henry James could not have been more wrong. I smell the ordure of envy in that pronouncement. The eminent critic George Steiner, in his marvelous book **Tolstoy or Dostoevsky,** praised the wizardry of both writers, but finally chose Dostoyevsky as the more important novelist because of his gift for darkness, and for identifying many of the psychological mysteries of the human spirit that would prove so relevant to the modern novel. Many American novelists have preferred the glorious **Anna Karenina** over **War and Peace,** and that includes William Faulkner, who, when asked about the greatest novel ever written, said, "**Anna Karenina, Anna Karenina, Anna Karenina.**" I will not argue with Mr. Faulkner only because **Anna Karenina** is the second-best novel I ever read.

The suicide of Anna still ranks as one of the saddest moments in world fiction.

Hundreds of people have written about **War and Peace** since its publication. Millions have read it. Tolstoy performs that rarest and most valuable of tasks, one that has all but disappeared from modern fiction. He wrestles with the philosophical issues of how people like you and me can manage to live praiseworthy and contributive lives. Reading Tolstoy makes us strive to be better people: better husbands and wives, children, and friends. He tries to teach us how to live by letting us participate in the brimming, storied experiences of his fictional world. Reading Leo Tolstoy, you will encounter a novelist who fell in love with his world and everything he saw and felt in it. His soul is a Russian soul, and he possesses the tireless generosity to give back to the world that made him vertiginous with a passion for life and nature—the gift that took the form of this miraculous, life-altering novel. Once you have read **War and Peace,** you will never be the same. That is my promise to you.

CHAPTER
THIRTEEN

MY TEACHER, JAMES DICKEY

Let me now praise the American writer James Dickey. I will make a few critical remarks about him, but that is only because he is dead, and I don't have to worry about him beating me up. It will also make me appear less sycophantic about Dickey's achievement; few people have loved his writing as much as I do. But let me begin with a statement of my own passionate and indignant belief—I do not care one goddamned thing about how James Dickey conducted his personal life. I care everything about what this man wrote on blank sheets of paper when he sat alone probing the extremities of his imagination. I don't care if James Dickey slept with a thousand women or the entire football team at Clemson or the marching band at Vanderbilt or every animal in the San Diego Zoo, including the duck-billed platypus, the Gaboon viper, or the last ivory-billed woodpecker on the planet. If Dickey had mated with a dozen lionesses on the Serengeti plain after they had killed a water buffalo, and a race of manticores had issued from the union, it would not make me love his writing less. Let us do the important thing—let us roar with laughter at his immense flaws as a man, but let us be sure not to forget his utter mastery of the English language as well as a literary gift as far-reaching and as prodigal as has ever appeared on the American scene.

Let me tell you a story that illustrates what my relationship with James Dickey was. There is not much of a story to tell, yet my first immersion in his poetry changed forever how I thought about writing. This happened when my friend Tim Belk threw me a copy of Dickey's **Poems *1957–1967***. Tim had attended a poetry reading in Savannah that Mr. Dickey had given the night before, and the poet had overpowered Tim with his mesmerizing, high-octane recital of his work. At the time, I was writing poetry that did small damage to the language, but added no glory to it whatsoever. I became intoxicated with the voice of James Dickey and said to myself, "I can't write like this. I'll never be able to write like this." But I read on for days until I had read every poem in the book. When I put it down I said finally, "I can't write. I just can't write."

Yet an admission of an inability to write

has never slowed down a certain American class of writer like me. To my surprise, I found out I couldn't live with my own mediocrity as a poet, so I turned to prose as an act of both surrender and self-knowledge. James Dickey had issued my marching orders and drummed me out of the poetry-writing world. On my desk, then and now, I keep his book of poems close to me, and I still turn to them for inspiration for their transcendental clarity, for their limitless passion—I turn to them to know what the English language is capable of when shaped and pulled and handled by a man born to set the world on fire. His poetry brought me to my knees then. It does the same thing to me today. Here was the truly amazing thing, I thought. At that time, James Dickey was still alive and teaching in my state.

In 1970 his novel **Deliverance** was published. I found it to be 278 pages that approached perfection. Every sentence sounded marvelous, distinct, and original, and it flowed as quickly as the river it celebrated. Its tightness of construction and assuredness of style reminded me of **The Great Gatsby.** Like his poetry, no line went in for showiness, no hint of laziness or inattention or loss of control. For me, Dickey had forged a palace of light for a white-water river of words.

When I finished the book, I said again to myself, "I can't write. I'll never be able to write like this."

This was not long after I had gotten myself fired from my teaching job on Daufuskie Island and had begun writing **The Water Is Wide,** which would eventually be published by Houghton Mifflin. I took it as a sign from God that the publishers of **Deliverance** would also be the publishers of my book, and I then thought it possible I might one day actually meet Mr. Dickey, shake his hand, and tell him what his writing had meant to me. So emotional was I about his work, I had to issue commands to myself not to genuflect and kiss his hand if we ever met. I didn't think he'd have liked it. After I met James Dickey, I think he might have assumed that the gesture was perfectly appropriate. At that time in my life, I did not know any writers, and I certainly did not consider myself one.

Because I was intoxicated by Dickey's work, I wrote a short story about cockfighting, one about a bombing raid over Hanoi, and one about a hunt for grizzly bears in Montana. I wrote three stories that brought shame and ridicule to the bright art of the short story and suddenly realized I had never been to a cockfight, never flown a plane over Hanoi, never been to Montana. I'd seen a grizzly bear only once, asleep at the National Zoo in Washington, D.C. Yet my entire writing career fueled itself with the mimicry of the great writers I loved the best, such as Thomas Wolfe, and I became skilled at grand larceny when it came to the theft of their ideas. I had no thoughts or style of my own when one of my best friends from high school, Jan Hryharrow, called to see if I wanted to take a canoe trip down the Chattooga River. I said yes in an instant, then realized I'd never been in a canoe. But in the full flower of my hero worship of James Dickey, I knew I must experience life lived on the edge, at its most dangerous extremes.

In Beaufort, I went out looking for a hunting rifle to bring on my trip down the Chattooga. When my wife, Barbara, questioned my sanity as to why anyone would take a rifle in a canoe, I told her that in the North Carolina mountains I would meet many mountain men who would try to have their way with me. "It's best to kill them with a bow and arrow," I said, "but I've never shot a bow and arrow, so I'm bringing a rifle."

"I think that's the dumbest thing I've ever heard a man say," Barbara responded.

"You haven't read **Deliverance,**" I said.

"And that sure as hell doesn't make me want to read it, either," she said.

When I remember this scene, it comes as no surprise that the marriage did not last.

So I went down the Chattooga rifleless with Jan Hryharrow, who told me he could take a six-month-old child down the river and the infant would not even get wet. He had bought the canoe from a YMCA camp for ten dollars, but refused to buy life jackets, which he considered overpriced. Jan was a river rat in Beaufort and an outdoorsman of considerable gifts—I trusted him completely until we came to the first white-water rapids, and I heard the thunderous noise of a waterfall ahead.

"Just keep stroking," Jan said. "No problem."

As we slid down the chute of the waterfall, I heard a scream and looked up to see Jan flying out, airborne above me as the canoe somersaulted in the air and I found myself engulfed in the boiling rapids. I lost my Citadel ring in that first waterfall, and I suspect it is still somewhere near there today. I also lost all respect and confidence in Jan Hryharrow as an outdoorsman. We capsized going over every single waterfall we tried to navigate that day. Never, not once, were Jan and I still in the canoe after trying to knife our way down the furious waterfalls of the Chattooga. Finally, we paused and rested before one that looked to me like Victoria Falls. It was called Sock-em Dog, and our waterproof map said more canoeists had been killed here than in any other part of the river. With irritating confidence, Jan told me he figured out what we were doing wrong. He had developed a new move, through trial and error, that would get us through Sock-em Dog unharmed. As we headed at a fearful pace toward our rendezvous with the most treacherous stretch of water on the river, Jan executed his new move with flawless precision. The canoe turned sideways and got suspended up on boulders. We were in a position as perilous as I have ever been in.

"Jan," I said as the waters roared around us, "I'd rather get raped by a mountain man than go down this river with you again."

"Get out onto the rocks," Jan said.

"Are you nuts?" I screamed.

"You've got to push us off. Then jump back in as fast as you can."

Resigned to my own death, I stood on the great rocks overlooking Sock-em Dog, pushed off, and watched Jan and the canoe get swept over the falls and disappear from sight. A quarter of a mile downstream they emerged. Shaken and dazed, Jan looked back and gestured with his hand and arm for me to join him.

"I'm going to die because James Dickey

wrote a novel," I thought as I jumped feet-first into the raging, man-killing water of Sock-em Dog. I am the only person I have ever known who swam the Chattooga River because he loved the literary work of James Dickey. Though it damaged my friendship with Jan, I had taken risks for the sake of my art. It gave me encouragement to write Mr. Dickey to ask if I could sit in on two of his courses the following year.

On January 9, 1972, I received this gracious reply from Mr. Dickey: **Dear Pat Conroy: Thank you for your recent note and for the things you were kind enough to say about my work. If you want to sit in on one of my classes, it's fine with me** (he underlined the word "me," giving me—not underlined—a cheap thrill), **but you'll have to take care of the administrative details with the English department, or whoever handles such things. Sincerely, James Dickey.**

I raced downtown to Edwards Department Store and bought a cheap black frame and put the letter in it. This letter remains emblematic and precious to me, and I have kept it near my desk for my entire writing career. I took it to Paris in 1979 and to Italy when I lived in Rome for three years in the eighties. I used it as a talisman and totem that my fate had straightened out in its course, and something ineffable and unalterable had come into my life. Now, at long last, I would learn whether I could swim the Chattooga or not. I began driving to Columbia twice a week to take Mr. Dickey's course in modern poetry and joined his poetry-writing workshop. James Dickey became my teacher.

Hero worship has always played an enormous role in my writing career. When I walked into James Dickey's class, I suffered from a terminal case of it, a goner beyond hope of redemption. I knew of no known antidote for my Dickey fixation, knew only that it was incurable. When a writer takes possession of me, there is nothing I can do but sit back and enter into the sacredness and delight of the ride itself. When James Dickey strolled into the room for that first class, I was dizzy with an exaltation I can still feel today. I had come to the place where I would learn how to write as I thought I was born to write. As he set his books down on the desk, I promised I would take in everything this poet had to say and would not waste a moment of his time. True to my word, I never spoke to Mr. Dickey in those two classes, but I wrote down every word he spoke. I never heard anyone read poetry with such authority or conviction. He made the English language seem like a tongue he had invented himself. In every way, he was a marvelous, passionate teacher, the kind that changes the lives of students who come to him for enlightenment. I would leave his classes and dance to my car, my head filled up with his words. As I drove back to Beaufort, I tried to force myself to think about language in the way James Dickey thought about it, or more thrillingly, the way my teacher thought about it.

From the beginning I had one great, roaring issue with the figure that James Dickey cut on the campus of the University of South Carolina. When Mr. Dickey first came into the classroom, it stunned me to see my father stroll into the room disguised as the greatest poet in the land. My hatred of my son-of-a-bitch father was in full flower when I came to Dickey's class, and no one whom I had ever met reminded me so much of Don Conroy. Both of them were large, intimidating physical presences; both had been accomplished athletes; both had found themselves as night fighters during World War II; and both exuded a masculinity that I found overpowering and even dangerous. Because I had been raised in the house of the Great Santini, beaten up badly on a regular basis, forced to play sports by a father who would always root for the other team to belittle me, then sent to The Citadel for a final ripening, I had encountered enough machismo in my life to start a Spanish restaurant. Dickey's mere aura could fill a room like a battleship, and his raw, animal physicality discouraged me from the beginning. I could even hear faraway hints of my father's commanding voice when Mr. Dickey spoke. I had never before met a poet, and think I had fantasized that James Dickey would teach me things like flower arranging or origami when I was hanging around after class. "This is the guy who wrote 'Falling' and 'The Heaven of Animals,'" I thought.

During my time with James Dickey I heard him read Dylan Thomas's poem "Fern Hill," and thought I had never heard a more beautiful male voice read a poem of such shimmering and immaculate language. I fell in love with a dozen poets just because I heard their work read with such devotional respect in that classroom. That winter, I attended the first James Dickey poetry reading I could get to, where my overwrought hero worship shifted into a much higher gear. Before that night, I thought poetry readings were the most torturous way of spending an evening outside of setting yourself on fire. I have never heard any writer, before or since, who read his own work with such inimitable skill, passion, or confidence. James Dickey was so amazingly good at these performances (I witnessed five of them) that I have never read from my own work. If I could not mesmerize a crowd in the Dickey way, I wanted no part of putting a crowd to sleep because I lacked his talent or charisma. He packed in the crowds, and they came to be transfigured. I had stumbled into Dickey's life at the most illuminating and perilous of times. James Dickey was in the process of becoming a celebrity, and I think it would partially ruin his life. That year, he talked often of Burt Reynolds and Jon Voight and the filming of **Deliverance.** I got to watch James Dickey fall in love with being James Dickey, and I believe this helped me as much as anything he taught me. I watched as Dickey became part of the newly developing celebrity culture in America, and I could sense its danger for him. I could hear the rapids ahead. He made it all sound glorious and romantic, this flirtation with Hollywood. All I could think of was, he was heading straight toward Sock-em Dog.

As I watched Mr. Dickey fall in love with his own fame that year, I worried about him. Because of my study of him, I decided never to teach writing in college if I could help it. It seemed deleterious to a man's character to have moon-eyed groupies such as me following you around campus, like a single file of box turtles. In class, I noticed that the other students were as gaga and reckless in their devotion to Dickey and his work as I was. I could not figure out how this would be desirable for the soul of a poet. The young women in the class were lovely and fresh and sometimes dazzling. These pretty girls would stare at Dickey with **Casablanca** eyes, the gorgeous eyes of Ingrid Bergman saying good-bye to Humphrey Bogart at the airport. It also occurred to me that those young women could offer Mr. Dickey a gift that I wasn't about to offer him, even if he was interested in accepting it. When visiting writers from other colleges came that year, I noticed a lot of sixty-year-old male writers married to twenty-year-old girls. Though I was fully capable of screwing up my own life in inscrutable and even unimaginable ways, it was important to learn about the pitfalls I could avoid if I were vigilant and cautious. James Dickey walked into a cathedral of worshipers whenever he came to class. It was great for us, his students, but when I left class on the final day, I had real doubts it was good for him.

I began serious work on **The Great Santini** while I was a student in Dickey's class. I also wrote a poem about a Little League coach I had one summer in Arlington, Virginia. Dave Murphy was an FBI agent who died a slow, agonizing death from cancer the year after he coached me. When I turned it in, I was mortally afraid, because by then I knew that Mr. Dickey could be a harsh and mordant critic. What I mean by that is that Dickey judged his students' work against the best poetry ever written. You either got better or got your feelings hurt rather badly. When he handed out the poems in the next class, he had written on mine: **Now we are onto something, Mr. Conroy. Now let's have at it. This is the real stuff. Now the real work begins.**

I left class armed with weaponry I needed for my own life among words. James Dickey and I never became friends, and I say that with regret, even sorrow. He treated me with genuine kindness whenever we met, which was not often. When **The Great Santini** was published, I had a signing where everyone could have fit into a telephone booth. But Maxine Dickey came and bought a book and treated me like visiting royalty. I had never met the wife of a great poet, but I've loved her my whole life for the kindness and class she showed me that day. She told me, "Jim's proud of you, but he'd never come to something like this. He's very competitive, you know."

"Having you come, Mrs. Dickey, is the

highest honor," I replied. "It's better than a visit from the ambassador from the court of St. James's."

I saw James Dickey very few times during the rest of his life. He sent me telegrams when my books or movies came out. I wrote him two letters in my life, thanking him from the bottom of my heart for his teaching and saying that I hoped I would prove myself worthy of that extraordinary time in his classroom. Then I talked about his writing and how much I admired it. Recently I returned to James Dickey's work. I didn't have to go far, since much of his work is on my writing desk. I read from **Poems *1957–1967*** almost every day of my writing life. **Sorties** is nearby and is wonderful. I booked a return passage on **Deliverance**. I reread **Self-Interviews,** dipped into **Alnilam** again (the badly titled novel that neither Mr. Dickey nor I could pronounce accurately). With joy, I went to **The Whole Motion** and **To the White Sea.** With nostalgia, I gave **The Zodiac** another chance and still feel it doesn't quite work. His output is enormous, and he wrote at a high level for a longer time than anyone else in the history of American letters. I would have loved to read the poetry he wrote in his late seventies and eighties. He kvelled with attention and praise. He bloomed in the limelight. Center stage was where he was born to be.

After I read the biography **James Dickey: The World as a Lie,** I was going to write a letter to its author, Henry Hart, and suggest that his next biography focus on the life of either Heinrich Himmler or Vlad the Impaler. Although I know why Henry Hart subtitled the book **The World as a Lie,** I think its essence would be served better by calling it **The World as a Myth,** or **The World as a Dream,** or **The World as a Poem**. What Mr. Hart misses with astonishing completeness is that art can never be a lie—even if James Dickey claims it is.

Will his work survive? Alas, I worry that it will not. As an American liberal with impeccable credentials, I would like to say that political correctness is going to kill American liberalism if it is not fought to the death by people like me for the dangers it represents to free speech, to the exchange of ideas, to openheartedness, or to the spirit of art itself. Political correctness has a stranglehold on academia, on feminism, and on the media. It is a form of both madness and maggotry, and has already silenced the voices of writers like James Dickey across the land.

Let me end my story with this: My relationship to James Dickey is a simple one. I go often to his mansion of art. To me, his book **Poems** *1957–1967* is the finest book of poetry ever published in America, and I include in that assessment **Leaves of Grass,** the collected works of Emily Dickinson, the works of Wallace Stevens, and I will throw in T. S. Eliot for dessert. When Dickey is writing at his best, it is like listening to God singing in cantos and fragments about the hard dreaming required for the creation of the world. Dickey crafts and fixes each of his sentences as though he were trying to shape a mountain range glorious enough to hover over Asia. When I read James Dickey, I am transported into that ecstatic country where poetry and poetry alone can take you and shake you with the cutting beauty and hammerlock of its language. Dickey changed the way I looked at mountain rivers, lifeguards, women preachers, flight attendants, wolverines, the belt of Orion, buck dancing, and a thousand other Dickey-praised subjects. His writing is mouthwatering, breathtaking, and our sweet-faced language had never packed as much bite and punch per pound as it did when James Dickey strung it to its bow and aimed it at the carotid artery of poetry itself. I can enter the world of his writing, and it is like swimming the Chattooga River. It is subtitled **The World as the Truth**.

One of the proudest moments of my life came years after James Dickey was my teacher, and that was when the Dickey family asked me to deliver James Dickey's eulogy. Here is my final prayer for James Dickey, and Dickey lovers will know where it comes from: Lord, let him die, but not die out.

WHY I WRITE

A novel is a great act of passion and intellect, carpentry and largesse. From the very beginning, I wrote to explain my own life to myself, and I invited readers who chose to make the journey with me to join me on the high wire. I would work without a net and without the noise of the crowd to disturb me. The view from on high is dizzying, instructive. I do not record the world exactly as it comes to me but transform it by making it pass through a prism of fabulous stories I have collected on the way. I gather stories the way a sunburned entomologist admires his well-ordered bottles of Costa Rican beetles. Stories are the vessels I use to interpret the world to myself. I am often called a "storyteller" by flippant and unadmiring critics. I revel in the title.

Many modern writers abjure the power of stories in their work, banish them to the suburbs of literature, drive them out toward the lower pastures of the lesser moons, and they could not be more wrong in doing so. But please, do not let me mince words in this chapter in which I offer an explanation and apologia for why I write. Fear is the major cargo that American writers must stow away when the writing life calls them into its carefully chosen ranks. I have been mortally afraid of the judgment of other writers and critics since I first lifted my proud but insecure head above the South Carolina marsh grass all those years ago. Some American writers are meaner than serial killers, but far more articulate, and this is always the great surprise awaiting the young men and women who swarm to the universities, their heads buzzing with all the dazzle and freshness and humbuggery of the language itself. My great fear of being attacked or trivialized by my contemporaries made me concentrate on what I was trying to do as a writer. It forced me to draw some conclusions that were my own. Here is one: The writers who scoff at the idea of primacy of stories either are idiots or cannot write them. Many of their novels could be used in emergency situations where barbiturates are at a premium and there has been a run on Unisom at the pharmacies. The most powerful words in English are "tell me a story," words that are intimately related to the complexity of history, the origins of language, the continuity of the species, the taproot of our humanity, our singularity, and art itself. I was born into the century in which novels lost their stories, poems their rhymes, paintings their form, and music its beauty, but that does not mean I had to like that trend or go along with it. I fight against these movements with every book I write.

Good writing is the hardest form of thinking. It involves the agony of turning profoundly difficult thoughts into lucid form, then forcing them into the tight-fitting uniform of language, making them visible and clear. If the writing is good, then the result seems effortless and inevitable. But when you want to say something life-changing or ineffable in a single sentence, you face both the limitations of the sentence itself and the extent of your own talent. When you come close to succeeding, when the words pour out of you just right, you understand that these sentences are all part of a river flowing out of your own distant, hidden ranges, and all words become the dissolving snow that feeds your mountain streams forever. The language locks itself in the icy slopes of our own high passes, and it is up to us, the writers, to melt the glaciers within us. When these glaciers break off, we get to call them novels, the changelings of our burning spirits, our life's work.

I have always taken a child's joy in the painterly loveliness of the English language. As a writer, I try to make that language pitch and roll, soar above the Eastern Flyway, reverse its field at will, howl and reel in the darkness, bellow when frightened, and pray when it approaches the eminence or divinity of nature itself. My well-used dictionaries and thesauri sing out to me when I write, and all English words are the plainsong of my many-tongued, long-winded ancestors who spoke before me. I write because I once fell in love with the sound of words as spoken by my comely, Georgia-born mother. I use the words that sound prettiest or most right to me as I drift into that bright cocoon where the writer loses himself in language. When finished, I adore the way the words look back at me after I have written them down on long yellow sheets. They are written in my hand, and their imperfect shapes thrill me. I can feed on the nectar of each word I write. Some are salt-rimed with the storm-flung Atlantic on them, some mountain-born, writhing in laurel, but each with a dark taste of my own life fresh upon it. What richer way to meet the sunlight than bathing each day of my life in my island-born language, the one that Shake-speare breathed on, Milton wrestled with, Jane Austen tamed, and Churchill rallied the squadrons of England with? I want to use the whole English language as the centerpiece of a grand alliance or concordance with my work. I see myself as its acolyte, its spy in the College of Cardinals, its army in the field. I try to turn each sentence into a bright container made of precious metals and glittering glass. It is the carrier and aqueduct of the sweet-est elixir of English words themselves. I build these sentences slowly. Like a glassblower, I use air and fire to shape the liquids as they form in my imagination. I long for that special moment when I take off into the pure oxygen-rich sky of a sentence that streaks off into a night where I cannot follow, where I lose control, when the language seizes me and shakes me in such a way that I feel like both its victim and its copilot.

Story and language brought me to the craft of writing; then passion and my childhood provided both the structure and the details. When I was busy growing up on the marine bases of my youth, my mother cast a spell on me that I found all but unbreakable. Peg Con-roy was rough-born and Southern-shaped, and I heard the stories of her Depression childhood so often that I have never been able to throw off the belief that I've known poverty inside and out from a very early age. I still hear my mother's voice, lovely beneath soft lamplight, whenever I sit down with a pen in my hand. She told me she was raising me to be a "Southern writer," though I have never been sure that she knew what that meant. My sister Carol listened to that same voice, heard those same stories, and became a poet as a result. Part of my childhood that is most vivid was being the chief witness to the shaping of an American poet in the bedroom next to mine.

My father was Chicago-born, and he brought the sensibilities of Augie March and Studs Lonigan to the cockpits of the fighter planes he flew over target areas along the coastal South. He was a pure man of action; he thought books made handsome furniture, but I never saw him read one. He raised me to be a fighter pilot like himself, and that is what I had planned to do before I was waylaid by literature. Yet my books have the feel of some invisible though embattled country, where the field artillery is always exchanging rounds between chapters. Like all battlefields, my novels fill up with smoke and noise and the screams of the wounded and the answering calls of medics low-crawling through the blasted, cratered fields with their canteens and their morphine ready. My father taught me the way of the warrior at the same time my mother was turning me into a wordsmith.

My parents taught me everything I needed to know about the dangers and attractions of the extreme. Even today, the purely outrageous to me feels completely natural. My novels reflect absurdity and the exorbitance of a house in which the fully unexpected was our daily bread. My father once wiped out a dozen tanks working their way toward marine lines in Korea, and my mother's hobby was collecting poisonous snakes. It is not my fault I was raised by Zeus and Hera, but my books mirror the odd, hothouse environment of my astonished childhood. All writers are both devotees and prisoners of their childhoods, and the images that accrued during those early days when each of us played out the mystery of Adam and Eve in our own way. My mother's voice and my father's fists are the two bookends of my childhood, and they form the basis of my art.

If my father's birthplace had been rural Georgia, and my mother had come up in South Chicago, I am positive that I would be known as a writer out of the Chicago school today. My mother was multiformed, hydra-headed, an untamable shape-shifter whose love of miscellany was a kind of ge-

nius. The women in my books all share an air
of mystery, an unwinnable allure that I trace
back to my inability to figure out what made
my mother tick. When I try to pin down her
soft, armor-covered spirit, when I fix it on a
slide beneath a microscope, I can feel it all
becoming immaterial before my steady gaze.
The colors rearrange themselves and the cos-
metology of her womanhood reverses itself.
My hunt will always be for my mother. She
could not give me herself, but she gave me
literature as a replacement. I have no idea
who she was, and I write my books as a way
of finding out.

My mother turned me into an insatiable,
fanatical reader. It was her gentle urging, her
hurt, insistent voice, that led me to discover
my identity by taking a working knowledge of the great books with me always. She
wanted me to read everything of value, and
she taught me to outread my entire generation, as she had done hers. I believe, and I
think fairly, that I have done that—that I
have not only outread my own generation of
writers but outread them in such a way that
whole secret libraries separate us. I have tried
to read two hundred pages every day of my
life since I was a freshman in high school, because I knew that I would come to the writing of books without the weight of culture

and learning that a well-established, confidently placed family could offer its children. I collected those long, melancholy lists of the great books that high school English teachers passed out to college-bound students, and I relied on having consumed those serious litanies of books as a way to ease my way into the literary life.

Even today, I hunt for the fabulous books that will change me utterly. I find myself happiest in the middle of a book in which I forget that I am reading, but am instead immersed in a made-up life lived at the highest pitch. Reading is the most rewarding form of exile and the necessary discipline for a novelist who burns with the ambition to get better.

Here is what I want from a book, what I demand, what I pray for when I take up a novel and begin to read the first sentence: I want everything and nothing less, the full measure of a writer's heart. I want a novel so poetic that I do not have to turn to the standby anthologies of poetry to satisfy that itch for music, for perfection and economy of phrasing, for exactness of tone. Then, too, I want a book so filled with story and character that I read page after page without thinking of food and drink, because a writer has possessed me, crazed me with an unappeasable thirst to know what happens next. Again, I know that story is suspect in the high pre-cincts of American fiction, but only because it brings entertainment and pleasure, the same responses that have always driven puritanical spirits at the dinner table wild when the talk turns to sexual intercourse and incontinence.

When an author sets the table right, there will be no need to pass either the foie gras or the barbecue because the characters will grab me by the collar. They will spring to life so fully developed, so richly contained in the oneness of their own universe, that they will populate the cafés and verandas and alley-ways of a city I will never want to leave. Few things linger longer or become more indwell-ing than that feeling of both completion and emptiness when a great book ends. That the book accompanies the reader forever, from that day forward, is part of literature's profli-gate generosity.

All through my life I have told myself—no, ordered myself—to read more deeply, read everything of consequence, let the words of some new writer settle like the dust of silica into the ledges and sills of my consciousness. When I find myself engaged in the reading of some magical, surprising book, I ask my-self these questions: Can I match this depth? Can I incorporate this splendid work, ingest it whole into my bloodstream, where it can become part of my thinking and dreaming life? What can this writer do that I can't? Can I steal the genius of this writer and learn all of the unappropriated lessons, then turn them into something astonishing that flows out of me because I was moved by the originality and courage and eloquence of another writer? Very early on, I set up for myself the endless task of reading and incorporating books of large and exuberant vision. By reading these luminous works, I learn the shy secrets of my craft, but I also gain some idea of the novel's fertility, its free-flowing immensity.

When I first sat down to write, I had to teach myself how to go about it. I called upon that regiment of beloved writers, living and dead, who had written the books that had changed the way I looked at myself and the world. I wanted the atmosphere of the novels to feel like the ones I had breathed in as a boy when I found myself in the grip of a mother-haunted imagination to which I owed both fealty and homage. I demanded living trees with actual names, flowers growing in their proper seasons, characters who spoke their minds, who lived as free men and women outside of my jurisdiction. My city of made-up people would live their own complex lives without my permission or my intrusion into their sovereignty. I wanted my fictional world to feel like the one I had grown up in, with no whitewashing of the horror that stood in the doorway of any given human moment. All my rivers had to be clean enough for the cobia, the herring, and the shad to swim upstream to spawn, because I was going back to my own sources to find the secrets of the world. I desired to be one of those writers who always followed the creek bed to that source, that clear pool where the mother's roe floated in still water above the glittering pebbles.

I promised myself nothing lazy would ever enter my books. Writing is both hard labor and one of the most pleasant forms that fanaticism can take. I take infinite care in how a sentence sounds to me. I rise out of the oral tradition of the American South, and words have to sound a certain way if they're to come out right.

In my first years, my identity as a writer was drawn toward amplitude, fullness, and extravagance. I worshiped writers who made me feel sated, coddled, spoiled with all the excess that too much attention and love can provide. The overreachers called out my name, and I responded with great zeal. I longed for writers to take me to the absolute crests and limits of their talents. I did not want them to leave out the grand tours of the abysses and spiritual Death Valleys they encountered along the way.

But since I have tried to read everything, I have also found that exactness is a virtue in even the most word-possessed writer. There is enormous power in stating something simply and well. Action sequences always require the straight line in the presentation, the most solid, sequential phrases, and the punchiest, most telling Anglo-Saxon sentences. Action brims and stirs. There is delicacy, craft, and restraint in all this, as in the making of a dry martini. But sometimes a lot more is required. Then you must go inside yourself to find the liftoff into the dark side of language's many rooms. When you have made a new sentence, or even an image that works well, it is a palace where language itself has lit a new lamp. It is why a writer sits alone, fingering memory and shaping imagination during the lost, solitary days.

As a writer, I have tried to make and remake myself over and over again. I try to notice everything, and if I take the time to write it, I would simply like to write it better than anyone else possibly could. If I am describing the Atlantic Ocean, I want to make that portion of the high seas mine forevermore, and I do not want the reader daydreaming about Herman Melville's ocean while getting a suntan on poor Conroy's. I try to be athletic and supple with my talent. I train it, urge it on, drive it to exceed itself, knowing in my bones that I need to be watchful about slippage, weariness, and running on empty. The safe writers have never interested me, do not excite a single shiver of curiosity within me. I can read five pages and know I am in the hands of a writer whose feet are cunningly placed on safe ground. Safety is a crime writers should never commit unless they are after tenure or praise. A novelist must wrestle with all mysteries and strangeness of life itself, and anyone who does not wish to accept that grand, bone-chilling commission should write book reviews, editorials, or health-insurance policies instead. The idea of a novel should stir your blood, and you should rise to it like a lion lifting up at the smell of impala. It should be instinctual, incurable, unanswerable, and a calling, not a choice.

I came to the writing life because my father's warplanes took off against me, and my mother's hurt South longed for her special voice. Nothing is more difficult for a writer to overcome than a childhood of privilege, but this was never a concern of mine. To experience a love that is too eloquent sometimes makes for a writer without edges. I have drawn long and often from the memory book of my youth, the local and secret depository where my central agony cowers in the limestone cave, licking its wounds, awaiting my discovery of it. Art is one of the few places where talent and madness can actually go to squirrel away inside each other.

I have used my books as instruments to force my way into the world. It was with surprise and wonder that I discovered that the same elemental, dangerous chemistry that moves through the volcanoes of the earth also moved through me. Through the words, I learned that life and art can be raised to a fever pitch, but the secret is in knowing when to reach for it. I want always to be writing the book I was born to write. A novel is my fingerprint, my identity card, and the writing of novels is one of the few ways I have found to approach the altar of God and creation itself. You try to worship God by performing the singularly courageous and impossible favor of knowing yourself. You watch for the black wings of fighters writing messages in the skies over the South. Your mother plays with snakes and poison and raises you to tell the stories that will make all our lives clear. It all congeals and moves and hurts in the remembering.

I can ask for nothing more.

CHAPTER FIFTEEN

THE CITY

I have built a city from the books I've read. There are thousands of books that go with me everywhere I go. A good book sings a timeless music that is heard in the choir lofts and balconies and theaters that thrive within that secret city inside me. I can walk the pleasure-giving streets of that illuminated, sleepless city anytime the compulsion strikes me, day or night. Some of the streets are fly-blown and unsafe, with chamber pots emptied on them by the housewives and butlers whose thankless labors allowed royals to be royal throughout the long reign of the printed word. If you follow me closely, I can guide you to alleyways of quartz, amethyst, and sunbaked rubies. I've developed a soft spot for overgrown, ruined gardens that offer safe nesting sites for vireos and orioles and tanagers. Ospreys dive for mullet in palm-lined lagoons, and a Serengeti plain allows the migrations of wildebeests through rivers teeming with crocodiles and hippopotamuses, with lions and warthogs and flamingos gathering at water holes in darkness. My city has bright aquariums, and the harbor linking it to the oceans of the world is heavy with the traffic of ships as a great white whale moves toward the setting sun; as Caesar makes up his mind about crossing the Rubicon; as Jesus of Nazareth blesses the bread and wine of his final seder feast; as an Icelandic poet composes a saga out of the primitive savagery of ice; as a cattle car is loaded in the train yards of Poland; as Rumi enters a trance of ecstatic life in Damascus. The stars whirl above in their ancient scrimmage of light, and everyone in my city notices their astonishing arrangement that lends a note of both order and chaos.

In the writing room of my Fripp Island house, there is a chapel of ease with my library rising in terraces and shelves all around me. For several months I've done little but think about the books I've read and collected over the years, the ones that have changed and challenged and elated me—along with the ones that disappointed in their execution or in some failure of conception. I require a solid judgment of good books to lead me to those unmarked lairs and secret bonfires that will clear the way to my own path of enlightenment. Ever since I was a child, I have read books to make me savvy and uncommon, and to provide me some moments of sheer divin-

ity where I can approach the interior border-
lines of ecstasy itself. Reading and prayer are
both acts of worship to me.

My mother promised that reading would
make me smart, and I found myself recruited
in Mom's battle over her own lack of a higher
education. She distributed books to me as
though they were communion wafers or the
tongues of fire that lit up the souls of the dis-
ciples with Pentecostal clairvoyance. Mom
would point her finger to a wall of books and
tell me she was showing me the way out of a
shame that was unutterable. I took whatever
book she put into my hand and made it part
of me. I made it the life of me, the essence of
my own tree of knowledge. With each book,
I built a city out of what my heart loved, my
soul yearned for, and my eyes desired.

Some of us read to ratify our despair about
the world; others choose to read because it
offers one of the only safety nets where love
and hope can find comfort. The subject of all
writers is the terrible brightness that wards
off the ineffable approach of death. I write
a poem in hopes that my name will lie fresh
on the tongues of language lovers a hundred
years from now; I write a novel in case a
poem is not enough. I create a city of fiction
because I want to leave an entire, considered
world behind me. When I open a window in

a town that I've made up in my head, I want
to make a world that readers can approach in
wonder.

Reading great books gave me unlimited access to people I never would have met, cities I
couldn't visit, mountain ranges I would never
lay eyes on, or rivers I would never swim.
Through books I fought bravely in wars of
both attrition and conquest. Before I'd ever
asked a girl out, I had fallen in love with Anna
Karenina, taken Isabel Archer to high tea at
the Grand Hotel in Rome, delivered passionate speeches to Juliet beneath her balcony,
abandoned Dido in Carthage, made love to
Lara in Zhivago's Russia, walked beside Lady
Brett Ashley in Paris, danced with Madame
Bovary—I could form a sweet-smelling corps
de ballet composed of the women I have loved
in books.

I learned how to be a man through the
reading of great books. Give me the courage
of Prince Andrei as he dresses for the Battle of
Borodino. Let me have one shot glass of the
courage that Robert Jordan displays at the end
of **For Whom the Bell Tolls**. Give me the
curiosity and resiliency of Garp, and a quest
so great that I would ride as a sidekick to Don
Quixote. Allow me to deliver the St. Crispin's
Day speech before the battle of Agincourt or
secrete myself into the wooden fretwork of

the Trojan horse. Give me a father like the one who raised Vladimir Nabokov in **Speak, Memory**, or one with the integrity of Atticus Finch, or the courage of Colonel Aureliano Buendía as he faced the firing squad in the immemorial first sentence of **One Hundred Years of Solitude**. Permit me to see the Lake Isle of Innisfree through the eyes of Yeats, or the infinite glories of Fern Hill through the sensibility of Dylan Thomas; the beaches of Chile as Pablo Neruda courted a gorgeous woman with a Spanish language that soared above them on a condor's wing.

I've always wanted to write a letter to the boy I once was, lost and dismayed in the plainsong of a childhood he found all but unbearable. But I soon discovered that I've been writing voluptuous hymns to that boy my whole life, because somewhere along the line—in the midst of breakdowns, disorder, and a malignant attraction to mayhem that's a home place for the beaten child—I fell in love with that kid. I saw the many disguises that boy used to ward off solitude, hallucination, madness itself. I believe that the reading of great books saved his life. At any time, I could take a sudden departure from the fighter pilot's house and find myself drifting through the tumult of Paris described in a book by Balzac. I could find myself on

Whitman's river-shaped Manhattan or be in Daisy Buchanan's arms when I woke up with a hangover in **The Great Gatsby**. I've used books to take me on journeys all over the world, to outer space, and to forbidden planets beyond. I've crossed the Arabian Desert with T. E. Lawrence; refreshed myself on an oasis in Morocco with Paul Bowles; gone up a treacherous African river with Joseph Conrad; lived deeply in Atlanta's Peachtree Road with Anne Rivers Siddons. I've traveled through Iraq with Freya Stark and . . . I could write like this forever. My city of books seems immeasurable and inexhaustible, and I can feel the others jumping up and down with their hands raised, demanding my attention, insisting that their voices be heard and their ballots counted.

When I lived in the heart of ancient Rome for three years in the 1980s, I would often go up to sit on the top step of Santa Maria in Aracoeli. Because I had read **The Education of Henry Adams**, I was well aware that Mr. Adams had sat in the same spot in silent homage to Edward Gibbon. Gibbon had lingered there as he took in the city's vast majesties while deciding to write **The History of the Decline and Fall of the Roman Empire**. When I walked to the church after I had finished my writing for the day, I'd read from one of the five volumes of Gibbon's masterpiece, knowing that I was occupying the same spot that sparked the great journey of Gibbon's life. I was then in the middle of writing **The Prince of Tides**, and I'd always take the time to pass through the grand entryway of the Palazzo dei Conservatori to stare at a piece of broken marble embedded in the wall across from the colossal head of Constantine. Earlier, two Englishwomen had pointed out the word "BRIT" in the surviving fragment; they informed me that this was the first mention of the island of Britain in world history. They reminded me that the language that was our common heritage was forming on the tongues of illiterate savages who had fallen before the implacable surge of the Roman legions. It remains a sacred moment in my life. That same week, the great American writer Gore Vidal showed me the exact spot where Julius Caesar fell after his assassination. For two years I paid the maintenance fees for the grave of Richard Henry Dana, the author of **Two Years Before the Mast**. He is buried in the Protestant cemetery along with John Keats, whose epitaph reads, "Here lies one whose name was writ in water."

Often at night I find myself drifting through my library of thousands of books and feel the lamps of wisdom light up the candelabras of my city of books. Deep within me, I've constructed elaborate museums and labyrinths from those writers whose complete works I have read over the years. Before I was twenty-five I had read every book that Charles Dickens wrote. Jane Austen came next, then Balzac, though I surrendered after I read half of his voluminous production. Wolfe, Faulkner, Fitzgerald, and Hemingway joined the reception line. When I bought a collection of Tolstoy and Dostoyevsky, I returned home with a bright enthusiasm to begin the long march into the Russian soul. Though I've failed to read either man to completion, they both helped me to imagine that my fictional South Carolina was as vast a literary acreage as their Russia. Then I entered my Henry James period, and I polished off **The Golden Bowl** to complete my study of his work. When Gene Norris lay dying in Newberry I spent the summer reading Anthony Powell's splendid collection **A Dance to the Music of Time.** Flannery O'Connor and Eudora Welty and Toni Morrison signed my dance card when the orchestra began to tune up in the main ballroom.

When I fell in love with a Dominican woman, she opened up to me a showy convention of Latin American writers from

Márquez to Borges to Vargas Llosa, and I read everything of those writers that had been translated into English. My attraction to Latin American literature led me to explore the rich literature of other countries, and I discovered the amazing world of Australian writers, which led me on a direct path to the teeming cities of India and the astonishing work of the Israeli writers, who then pointed me in the direction of Cairo, where I encountered the Egyptian world of the Nobel Prize winner Naguib Mahfouz.

In a reading life, one thing leads to another in a circle of accident and chance. When I found a copy of Italo Calvino's **The Baron in the Trees** on a bench in Central Park, I remembered meeting him at a coffee bar in Rome, but the encounter was so low-key that I didn't rush out to find his work. Once I did, he became one of my favorite writers. His **Invisible Cities** strikes me as a masterpiece of the first order. The book is a long epic poem, a glittering tour de force, an extinct volcano that comes roaring back to explosive life, a code of conduct into the mind's interior realms, a delight and a paradox. I can't pass a bookstore without slipping inside, looking for the next book that will burn my hand when I touch its jacket, or hand me over a promissory note of such immense power that it contains the formula that will change everything about me. Here is all I ask of a book—give me everything. Everything, and don't leave out a single word.

The poets of the world occupy a place of high honor in my city of books. Those wizards of language draw me into the vast acreage of their talent. A book of poetry is made up of threads that coil around the soft bodies of sound. Stealing the linens of the spoken word, poets are not shy about displaying the rose windows and altar cloths of their prodigious art. When they arrive at my city gates, they clamor for entrance and scream out their poems to me from outside the city walls. I go to the poets often for their comfort in the maelstrom of their imaginations. Some of them write with a monastic clarity and simplicity that reduces art to its very essence. I prefer the poets who roll up their sleeves to show me intricate tattoos of peacocks and dragon-ravaged towns and clowns playing glockenspiels. Each day before I begin to write, I choose a poet to keep on my desk. Poets candle the pilot light where language hides from itself.

In other moods and other hours, I carry a keen desire for those poets who know how to trim the fat with blades turned deadly with whetstone. These are the poets who use language so sparingly they can nail your hand to a doorway. Each word comes to you hard-earned and deboned, flayed and boiled down to its essence. These astringent poets keep their tool belts full of instruments that carve and cut and sort. Cavafy writes poems of this nature and doesn't clear his throat or raise his voice as he spreads his whole world on the table for inspection. William Carlos Williams became famous for his championing of a poem being as simple and lovely as a string of pearls. With all poets, it comes down to how they put words together and the effect those words have. Though they struggle to make a living, poets will always have the last word about how the language is shifting as we move into a distraught, rustled future. I like poets to light their fires, granting me permission to begin my own work for the day.

Across from where I write, I keep a strong-shouldered squad of poets at my beck and call. Though there is a frequent changing of the guard, I try to find the clearest, most mesmerizing voices to jump-start me into creation. These poets wink at me, knowing that I am praising them. It begins with **The Beauty Wars**, my sister Carol's lyrical collection. Rumi, red-jacketed and whirling, follows my sister in his trancelike devotion to the dance of language. The next marksman in my squad is the sad-faced Federico García Lorca, shouldered against Wallace Stevens and Geoffrey Hill. Lisel Mueller is dancing with Eugenio Montale while Dylan Thomas is offering James Dickey a whiskey at the White Horse Tavern. Executing an about-face, I come up to inspect the tricorn hat of Marianne Moore, who is dressing herself for a windswept walk across the Brooklyn Bridge with her drinking buddy, Hart Crane. Three poetry books form a strong line of defense at the end of the squad: an anthology of Latin American poetry, the complete poems of Borges, and the collected works of Pablo Neruda. A young man or woman could take that string of books, study them with no small degree of fanaticism, and spend a far richer year than they ever did at a university.

Each day of my life begins with a poem that will unloose the avalanche of words inside me, that secret ore that, once polished, will sit before me disguised as the earth's jewelry. I'll select from its garnets, its milky-eyed opals, its insect-killing amber—it's the language I revere above all. I cheer when a writer stops me in my tracks, forces me to go back and read a sentence again and again, and I find myself thunderstruck, grateful the way readers always are when a writer takes the time to put them on the floor. That's what a good book does—it puts readers on their knees. It makes you want to believe in a world you just read about—the one that will make you feel different about the world you thought you lived in, the world that will never be the same.

I return a final time to my city of literature, my honored city of books, and the glittering city of words that greets me as I walk through my library. On my desk lies a treasure sent to me by the bookseller Chan Gordon, who runs an excellent bookshop in Asheville, North Carolina. From his desk at the Captain's Bookshelf, Chan has presented me with an exquisitely printed elegy by Thomas Meyer mourning the death of the poet Jonathan Williams. The pages are handmade, and the slender volume looks as though it might have been milled with butterfly wings and the armored enamel of ladybugs. The title of the poem is taken from an obscure yet enchanted Japanese word, **kintsugi**. When I read the title, I thought I'd been reading my whole life waiting to stumble upon this spellbound word camouflaged in the bonsai ferneries of a foreign language. "**Kintsugi**" is "the Japanese practice of repairing ceramics with gold-laced lacquer to illuminate the breakage." Ah, I thought, there is no attempt to hide the breakage—that golden, beautiful lacquer emphasizes the harm to the crockery or stemware. As Thomas Meyer bids farewell to the poet, he turns his words into a gold fluid that hardens along the fault lines that are ending the poet's life. Because I love to read, Thomas Meyer comforts me over the loss of Jonathan Williams and offers me a deep shell of metaphor that I can use to help explain my own writing to myself. Though I have always known that pain was a ham-fisted player in my novels, I didn't understand that I had used the radiant lacquers of the language to mark the wounds and fissures I had forced upon my characters. Though I was aware I hurt and damaged many of the characters I'd grown to love in my books, I never knew I practiced the subtle art of **kintsugi** until Thomas Meyer let me in on the secret.

In Vienna in 1982, I was met at the train station by the American novelist Jonathan Carroll. Someone had sent him a copy of **The Lords of Discipline**, and he'd liked it enough to invite me to visit him. He'd also sent me an inscribed copy of his book **The Land of Laughs**, and I received it with much excitement. His penmanship was lush and wondrous, and he drew pictures of bull terriers next to his autograph. When I read the book, I entered into such a strange and oddball country of the spirit that I was thrown off. Then the magic happened, the feeling I always wait for, as the book began to launch itself into orbit. I found myself in perfect congruity with the navigator and started trusting the narrator's insistent voice. Since that first book, I've read every book that Jonathan Carroll has published, from **Bones of the Moon** and **A Child Across the Sky** to **White Apples**. I've read no other writer like him, because there is no other even remotely similar. Anything goes in his books. In America, I once called him a cult waiting to be born. In Poland, thousands line up for his autograph. He's the kind of guy who wins the Nobel Prize at the end of his life when no one in his native land even knows his name.

On my first night in Vienna, Jonathan walked me down to the Danube, where we sat on a flight of steps leading down to the river. The dog walkers were out in force. Greetings were exchanged with small movements of the eyes, and the dogs sniffed one another fondly. Handsome and imperial, Jonathan looked every inch the American expatriate. He exuded a serenity and a seriousness that I lack. But he kept his eye on a woman at the next bridge. She was moving so slowly I thought she might be leading a dogsled pulled by escargots. After an hour, the woman walked in front of us, and she bowed her head in acknowledgment of Jonathan. With great dignity, he returned the gesture. To my surprise, she was walking two enormous tortoises, displaced natives from an Ethiopian desert. The woman walked them every night, and Jonathan was always there to admire their passage.

"That's what writers do, Conroy," he said. "We wait for the tortoises to come. We wait for that lady who walks them. That's how art works. It's never a jackrabbit, or a racehorse. It's the tortoises that hold all the secrets. We've got to be patient enough to wait for them."

ACKNOWLEDGMENTS

To my beloved wife, Cassandra King, who writes her books upstairs as I write mine downstairs. She has brought harmony and peace and joy into my life, and I'll never be able to thank her enough for finding me in Birmingham, Alabama.

To my irreplaceable friend, Doug Marlette, who introduced me to the Florida novelist Janis Owens, who in turn has helped explain my mother's life to me. The entire Owens-Johnson clan has embraced me as a new member of the family. All praise to Wendell Owens and the beautiful daughters, Emily, Abigail, and Isabel; the scrumptious Lily Pickle; and to Roy and Martha, Jay and Jeff Johnson.

To Bernie Schein, my childhood friend and north star, who has been the closest companion and head cheerleader of my writing career. To Martha Schein, Maggie, Lara Alexander, Aaron and Nancy Schein. And in memory of Morris and Sadie Schein.

To my brothers and sisters, my boon companions through the firestorm of our youth: Carol Ann, Michael, Kathleen, Jim, Tim, and in memory of Tom.

To my Alabama family: Elton, Beckie, Nancy Jane, Jim, Jason, Jacob, and all the rest.

A gleam of pride for my daughters: Jessica, Melissa, Megan, and Emily.

A hurrah for our rowdy, inexhaustible houseful of grandchildren: Elise, Stella, Lila, Wester, Molly Jean, Jack, and Katie. Then there are Alessandra, Alina, Tyler, Michael, Sophia, Henry, and Anna Jane.

To the rocks of my publishing life: Nan and Gay Talese, Stephen Rubin, Marly Rusoff, Mihai Radulescu, Julian and Hope Bach, Carolyn Krupp, Jonathan Galassi, Todd Doughty, Lauren Lavelle, Elizabeth Johnson, Anne Rivers Siddons, Terry Kay, Ron Rash, Josephine Humphreys, Dottie Frank, and with a loving bow to Anne Torrago, who has been with me every step of the way.

To all the reps of my publishing life. I loved it when we took to the road together to sell books, to talk about books, and to celebrate our world of books together.

Finally, to the friends along the way: John and Barbara Warley, Scott and Susan Graber, Cliff and Cynthia Graubart, Tim Belk, Alex

and Zoe Sanders, Jim Landon, Carol and
Blake Young, Gregg and Mary Wilson Smith,
Jay and Anne Harbeck, Coach Ed Conroy
of Tulane University, and the family of Julia
Randel.

About the Author

Pat Conroy is the author of nine previous books: **The Boo, The Water Is Wide, The Great Santini, The Lords of Discipline, The Prince of Tides, Beach Music, My Losing Season, The Pat Conroy Cookbook,** and **South of Broad.** Several of his books have been made into successful films. He lives in Fripp Island, South Carolina.